INSTAGRAM

How to Crack the Instagram Algorithm

(Network Marketing and Personal Branding Strategies)

Nancy Lamb

Published by Andrew Zen

Nancy Lamb

All Rights Reserved

Instagram: How to Crack the Instagram Algorithm (Network Marketing and Personal Branding Strategies)

ISBN 978-1-989965-83-2

Legal & Disclaimer

The information contained in this book is not designed to replace or take the place of any form of medicine or professional medical advice. The information in this book has been provided for educational and entertainment purposes only.

The information contained in this book has been compiled from sources deemed reliable, and it is accurate to the best of the Author's knowledge; however, the Author cannot guarantee its accuracy and validity and cannot be held liable for any errors or omissions. Changes are periodically made to this book. You must consult your doctor or get professional medical advice before using any of the suggested remedies, techniques, or information in this book.

Upon using the information contained in this book, you agree to hold harmless the Author from and against any damages, costs, and expenses, including any legal fees potentially resulting from the application of any of the information provided by this guide. This disclaimer applies to any damages or injury caused by the use and application, whether directly or indirectly, of any advice or information presented, whether for breach of contract, tort, negligence, personal injury, criminal intent, or under any other cause of action.

You agree to accept all risks of using the information presented inside this book. You need to consult a professional medical practitioner in order to ensure you are both able and healthy enough to participate in this program.

Table of Contents

INTRODUCTION.. 1

CHAPTER 1: WHAT'S YOUR "WHY"? 2

CHAPTER 2: THE DIFFERENCE BETWEEN INSTAGRAM AND
OTHER SOCIAL MEDIA SITES... 5

CHAPTER 3: THE BENEFITS OF USING INSTAGRAM FOR
BUSINESS 19

CHAPTER 4: TIPS AND TRICKS FOR UNSTOPPABLE
CAMPAIGNS 32

CHAPTER 5: ORGANIC TRAFFIC AND GROWING YOUR PAGE
.... 46

CHAPTER 6: YOU MUST FOLLOW THESE LAWS FOR
WRITING YOUR BIO IN ORDER TO INSTANTLY GENERATE
POTENTIAL BUYERS, NOT SIMPLY FOLLOWERS................. 87

CHAPTER 7: HOW TO USE INSTAGRAM WITH YOUR DIRECT
SALES BUSINESS 99

CHAPTER 8: THE PROS AND CONS OF INTERNET
MARKETING 122

CHAPTER 9: HOW TO CREATE A BRAND STORY WITH
INSTAGRAM 138

CHAPTER 10: HOW TO MAKE MONEY USING INSTAGRAM.

.... 141

CHAPTER 11: CONVERTING YOUR FOLLOWERS TO CLIENTS

.... 157

CHAPTER 12: TIPS FOR CREATING HIGH-QUALITY CONTENT

FOR YOUR INSTAGRAM... 165

CONCLUSION... 190

Introduction

Thank you for the purchase of this book. If you are looking to make your way into the world of online marketing, specifically marketing on Instagram, then this is the book for you. Instagram is one of the most popular social media sites that are out there today. Loving the ease of sharing life's moments with photos, millions of people frequent it each day. This makes it a great fit for you to market your product.

Of course, you are going to need to know the inner workings of Instagram, and how to post and share at just the right times in order to gain the biggest following. You are also going to need to know how to make a profit, and this book contains all of that information and more. Enjoy!

Chapter 1: What's Your "Why"?

"I've always been a bit of an introvert, but just because you don't fit the classic mold doesn't mean you can't be a leader. You just need to find your own style and someone with a similar style who you can learn from." - Jess Lee

Instagram has become a competitive space and there are over 1 billion people using the platform every month. You need to fight for the attention of these users - Don't expect to throw up a meaningless post with a few emojis and suddenly you'll see a spike in sales. Your account needs to stand out from the crowd.

THE FACTS:

• 200 million Instagram users visit at least one business profile daily.

• Instagram's potential advertising reach is 849.3 million users.

- 75.3% of US businesses will use Instagram by the end of 2020.

- 63% of users log in at least once per day.

- 62% of people say they have become more interested in a brand/product when they see it on Instagram stories

- Instagram is the second most downloaded free app in the Apple app store

The statistics here make it clear - there are people on this platform and you need to make sure your business is there too. But if you want to really start generating sales from Instagram, you need to understand your "why" and start providing value to your audience.

Why do people follow you? What's your point of difference? What value do you provide? What does someone get out of following you? It's important that your focus always remains on the customers wants or needs - your Instagram should be about them, not you.

If you are not providing a value or meaning to your Instagram account, you fail to create a connection with your followers and not only will they not purchase from you, it's likely they will unfollow you all together.

Start asking yourself these questions and brainstorm what you'd want to see on Instagram everyday if you were one of your customers.For example, as a social media manager, I share lots of tips on how to grow your business online, hacks to use on Instagram and behind the scenes content of my day-to-day life as a business owner. This can apply to any business, both product and service based.

These are ideas that we are going to explore further in the next few chapters, but I wanted to start by making sure your brain is ready to think outside the box and you understand what your Instagram is all about.

Chapter 2: The Difference Between Instagram And Other Social Media Sites

There are so many different social media sites that are out there and all of them promise to bring you the customers and sales that you want. But all of them are going to work in slightly different manners, so sometimes it depends on the kind of customer that you are trying to reach when it comes to which of the social media sites that you would like to work with. Let's take a look at how Instagram compares to some of the other social media sites that you may have used in the past and see how it can make a difference in your business.

Facebook

Facebook is an online social networking service that was launched in 2004. It allows you to meet up with friends and family and share pictures, videos, and blog posts about what is going on in your life. It is possible to have your own personal page on this site or you can create a new page that is professional and just for your business. This social media site can be accessed by tablets, smartphones, computers, laptops, and desktops. You can create a profile for Facebook and then indicate some information about yourself or your business so that others are able to find you.

Often businesses are going to start their own business sites, which you can do through a separate account or have it attached to your personal account so they are all in one place. You can share this information on your marketing materials so that others can find you and keep up to date on what is going on in your business.

This is a great place to be interactive with your customers, using videos, promotions, and pictures along with your blog posts to share information.

Facebook can do quite a few of the same things that you find on Instagram, but it often relies more on text and blog posts than you will find with Instagram. You should still make sure that your posts are interactive and fun for your customers and take the time to fill out your business profile, complete with a good name and picture for your customers to find you.

Twitter

Twitter is another great social media site that businesses have come to use to help themselves grow. This one was launched in 2006 and as of 2012, there were more than 100 million users on this site, which provides you with many followers who may be interested in your information. this is a great website if you want to reach your customers in a quick and efficient manner, but you will be limited to writing out posts that are 140 characters or less.

This one is good if you want to post links to your website or other useful information, but you need to be creative order to fit into the small character count that is allowed. You can add in some pictures, but this is not the most effective method for posting pictures of your business. If you want a social media site that is really picture oriented and great for showcasing the products and services that are available on your website, this is not the one for you.

Pinterest

Pinterest is another photo sharing website that is going to rely quite a bit on pictures. The founders of this company state that Pinterest is like a catalog of ideas rather than having it there for social networking. This is a good site to use to really showcase the pictures that you have in pins on your different boards. You can take high-quality pictures of your products with some little descriptions. You can add in your website so that people can go there to check out more information and decide whether or not to purchase the products.

With this one, you do need to come up with some high-quality pictures to make others want to choose you over someone else. You need to have some good keywords in place so that your potential customers are able to find you and look at your products to purchase them.

The benefit of Instagram over Pinterest is that right now Pinterest doesn't really have the capabilities for videos that you can find with Snapchat and Instagram. There are a lot of great things that you can do with pictures on this one, but Instagram has more of the conversion rate that you want compared to Pinterest and since you are able to add in some videos on occasion to make it stand out, Instagram is often the best one that you can use.

Snapchat

Snapchat is a bit different because it is more about multimedia and image messaging. One of the ideas behind this social media app is that the pictures and the messages are going to be available for just a short period of time because they can't be found any longer. This one can be a little bit tough for some businesses because you have to send out messages that have a lot of power behind them that only last a few seconds before they are gone. This means that they don't have any staying power; you won't be able to keep showing them over and over again or have your customers share the information to become viral. But it can be a unique method of social media that you can use if you need something a little bit new.

Most business marketers are going to choose to skip out on this one even though there are many customers who are on it. It is kind of hard to create content all the time when it is going to just disappear.

You will want most of your messages to stick and to have the ability to be shared with others across the media site. But if you create a message and then it is deleted shortly afterward, it is hard to have a lot of people see it. Most marketers want some more staying power and this means that it is best to go with some other options on social media.

Instagram

As you can see, some of these social media accounts will be similar to what you can do with Instagram. Some of them allow you to share pictures while others are better for doing videos or blogging. But with Instagram, you are focusing on creating content that is going works well in picture and video format. The better quality you are able to get these media on your account, the easier it is to attract your customers and get them to at least take a look at your site rather than just passing you by.

There are many great social media accounts that you are able to pick but when it comes to growing your business and reaching your customers in a way that really works to convert their views into sales, Instagram is one of the best options that you can choose.

How to Create Your Own Business Account on Instagram

Now that we know a bit more about Instagram, it is time to get your own business account set up. Some beginners may try to use their own personal account, if they have one, in order to work on their business, but this is not a good idea. If you have one account for your personal stuff and your business stuff at the same time, you are going to lose some of your professionalism for the account and can really confuse the clients that you are working with. It is never a good idea to have these combined. You can have a personal account, but you also need to consider having a new account that is just for your business.

So the first step that you need to set up this account is to define how you are going to use Instagram to serve the business. There are a lot of business objectives that you will be able to meet when you use Instagram and it is great for many different businesses, but if you would like to succeed, you need to make sure that you narrow your focus. You need to pick some of the things that you want to focus on and then stick with consistent posting and high-quality content to bring in the customers.

From here, you can go to the main login page for Instagram and sign up for a new account. You will want to think carefully about the username that you will put with this. You want the name of the account and the username to match with your business as much as possible (if someone already has the name exactly, you may need to make some adjustments). Make sure to have a strong password in place to help keep the information about your business safe.

Now you need to add in a description, which will be your bio and needs to be no more than 150 characters. Use this space wisely to describe what your business is all about and what this channel is for. This is not the place to get into a ton of details because you are limited on space, but make it interesting to get the customers in.

In the bio section, you will not be allowed to post links to your website on the individual posts (so you can't link to your website later in some of the posts), so the bio section is a good place to put this so that your customers know where to find you. Don't waste this on the homepage. You should also take the time to update this link often, especially if you end up having events, special promotions, and big product launches.

Unlike some of the other social media sites that you may choose to work with, Instagram isn't going to have the option of a custom photo on the cover to help you out with some of the brand recognition. This means that if you want to work on branding, you will need to do so with the content that you publish on your feed so make sure that you are planning wisely.

It has been pretty recent when Instagram started introducing business profiles, which can help out because it allows you to provide a business address, industry, and contact information on the profile. Instagram also has the option to use analytics so that you can take a look at who your followers are and how they behave.

Make sure to fill out all the different parts that come with your Instagram business account. There are so many aspects that can come into play with this and the more information that you post, the easier it is going to be to show your customers what you are all about. Fill out the industry and the bio, make sure that you put in the link to your website, and post some high-quality content so that others are easily able to find you.

Remember that with this account, you need to conduct yourself as a business. Make sure that you are posting things that relate to your business and the products or services that you sell. Make sure that you leave the personal stuff out of the mix and learn how to interact and form the right relationships. It is going to take some time to build all of this up and start to get some of the results that you want, but it is just like some of your other social media accounts and you just need to keep going to get the results that you want.

Chapter 3: The Benefits Of Using Instagram For Business

The increasing popularity of social media makes it a matter of urgency and utmost importance for your business to be advertised on these platforms if you are really serious about creating a viable funnel for directing traffic to your business and gradually growing it.

If you have chosen to promote your business on Instagram, what do you stand to gain from that decision?

There are some valuable benefits you can derive from driving your business growth with Instagram. Let's have a look at some of the best benefits you can derive from it:

Increased engagement

While many brands concentrate on using Twitter and Facebook to increase their online engagement with their customers, they oftentimes overlook the potential of

Instagram to help increase their engagement. If you have an active Instagram account with valuable content, you have a platform that can increase your engagement levels beyond your imagination.

If you have a new product or service, sharing such information and asking people's opinion about them is a great way to leverage the better engagement to your own benefit. You can equally give your followers a sneak peek into the future of a new project and welcome their input. You may find your followers' input more valuable to the success of the new project.

You can build trust and personality

One of the easiest ways for brands to generate more engagement is to promote their products with branded content. With Instagram, you can easily leverage the power of your branded content to build a lasting trust amongst your followers. If you can work hard to establish a strong emotional connection with your followers, you will benefit from that feature of Instagram.

If you have a specific brand that you want to promote on the platform, you need to have some amazing ways to promote them to build a good relationship with your audience. One of the methods is by using some behind-the-scene photos. The community usually appreciates employee images if they are professionally shot and are high-quality. Such beautiful images will pass the right information to the community.

The more of such photos you post on your page, the more Instagramers will show interest in your posts. As a result, you can have a good shot at portraying your company in a good light; you increase the company's attractiveness and trustworthiness. That in the long run will impact your business positively as more people become aware of it.

You can reach your target audience

Instagram may be the perfect place where you can reach your target audience. If your brand is targeting young people, you have an abundance of them on Instagram. A recent study by Jenns Trends shows that almost 4 out of every 10 adults under the age of 30 can be found on Instagram. So, if you are targeting people within that age group, you shouldn't hesitate to create an Instagram account.

It also attends to the needs of other groups of people as well. A study by Inc.com showed that since 2012, the number of adult Instagram users in the United States has doubled since more adults are getting used to Instagram and a good percentage of the young users are coming of age.

You should try to find out the age group that your brand is targeting and use the right tools, either by Instagram or by a third party, to target your audience. That will boost your chances of reaching your target market on the platform. Regardless of your target audience, you will always find a ready audience on the platform.

Free advertisement

Advertising, if done right, is crucial to the success of every business. It is one of the most powerful and effective strategies to create awareness to your audience. It has been used for decades for increasing the popularity of a brand. Many companies depend on advertising for their success and have benefited immensely from that decision. That makes it worthwhile to consider the fact that you have access to free advertising.

Instead of contemplating how to raise a small fortune for paid advertisements anywhere, you can enjoy the free advertisement offered by Instagram to increase your reach and gradually build your business, exactly what paid advertisements hope to achieve.

By updating your page regularly with valuable content and attractive photos with the right attributes, your popularity on social media will take a huge leap. In no time, you will reach as many people as you want without spending excessive amounts of money on paid advertising.

This is good news for business owners who are running their businesses on a shoestring budget. Without worrying yourself about how to raise advertising capital, a few minutes are sufficient for you to sign up to an Instagram account and start the race of building huge followers for your account.

Increased traffic

This is the major reasons why you have an Instagram account. You want to leverage the services it offers you to build a large portfolio for yourself on the media, all while you drive referral traffic to your website.

Despite the fact that you can directly add clickable links to your posts, it is still a very powerful and result-oriented way to drive an amazing amount traffic to your website. A platform that offers you a higher engagement level than that of Twitter and Facebook has the potential to give you sufficient traffic to keep your business afloat. You only need to do two things: create an impressive bio and do your best to maintain the profile. Don't forget the valuable impact that updating your page with valuable content has. You must leave no stone unturned in your attempt to get your followers addicted to your posts. That will make them pledge their total allegiance to you.

It offers competitive advantage

If you are an active member of Twitter and Facebook, you will realize that Instagram has less competition compared to those platforms. The implication is that you have a very powerful platform for showcasing your business or brand without the crazy competition you must contend with on both Twitter and Facebook.

The reduced levels of competition on Instagram should be put to good use by capitalizing on the freedom and have less competition so you can expand your reach to as many people as possible.

A recent study by the American Express survey indicated that about 2% of small scale businesses operate on Instagram. That reduces your competition, and you can leverage such reduced competition to create more awareness for your business rather than spend a huge chunk of your time fighting the stiff completion.

It is ideal for different business sizes

You don't need to entertain unnecessary worry over the size of your business. Instagram is designed to cater to the needs of different companies and brands regardless of the size of their staff.

While some big brands have taken their awareness and popularity to a whole new level, small brands are not left behind. They have mastered the use of the platform to get the most out of it. It is not unusual to see both brands succeeding on the platform by taking advantage of the accommodating nature of the platform.

Some of the big brands that have found success on Instagram include:

Audi: This auto company is one of the leading names in the auto industry. In recent years, Audi has taken to Instagram to promote its line of cars. The result has been impressive. In just 90 days, two of its photos generated 104,000 and 109,000 interactions respectively. This is an indication that the auto company knows the rules and is applying them correctly.

The company used some catchy captions to attract the attention of their followers.

Starbucks: This is another company that has the know-how of using Instagram to garner engagements. Within a period of two-and-a-half months, the company made 77 posts. With these posts, Starbucks received in excess of 20 million engagements. This is an average of over 270,000 engagements for each of their posts. The most engaging of these posts is the Lemonade post. This post received over 2,000 comments and about 400,000 likes. During that period, the company gained about 1.5 million new followers which translated to a 180% engagement increase.

Nike: Nike is one of the most popular sportswear manufacturers in the world. Over the course of years, this giant company has used its experience and high-quality images to drive traffic in droves to its Instagram account.

According to a recent study of the biggest brands on Instagram with the highest number of followers, Nike is ranked second, below only to National Geographic.

It is expected that this figure will continue to rise as the company keep playing the game by the rules. With an apt caption, attention-grabbing images, and the other factors, more followers will keep identifying with this sportswear giant.

If you are apprehensive about taking your chances with Instagram, you should consider using Nike's tagline as a piece of advice: Just do it.

Similarly, some small brands have equally benefited from Instagram as I highlighted above. Therefore, the size of your brand is never an excuse for missing out on the plethora of benefits that Instagram offers businesses.

The earlier you commit your business to Instagram, the earlier you benefit from it.

Your brand will feel the positive impact of such a wise decision.

Chapter 4: Tips And Tricks For Unstoppable Campaigns

Instagram is going to be a home for your brand's advertising and marketing efforts for a very long time. In fact, with the numbers and percentage of users and businesses increasing each year, this social media platform isn't going to go away anytime soon. This platform is the ideal place for businesses to engage with the audiences and customers, to reach out and bring in new customers and to build that lasting connection which is so vital to the survival of the business. Without your customers, your business would not exist, which is why it is important for a business to reach out to their customers in every way possible. Social media platforms like Instagram, just make it much easier to do so.

As with every other marketing campaign, the ones you conduct on Instagram must have a specific goal and objective that you are trying to achieve. Your campaign should exist for a reason, a purpose that you're focused on making a reality. This objective and goal that you have set, should be something that is measurable so you know that it is worth your time and your effort. All that energy that you're putting into your campaign should yield results to make it an unstoppable, successful campaign.

Building brand awareness and loyalty is a slow and steady race on Instagram. Advertising and marketing campaigns, however, are like sprints. Happens every now and then, for a short burst of time and produces quicker, focused and targeted results. For example, if your brand is looking at launching a new product, or driving awareness amongst new customers, then an unstoppable Instagram campaign is going to be what you need to achieve that goal.

Instagram is loved by businesses and marketers, and it is easy to see why. Forrester conducted a study which found that Instagram had an engagement rate of 4.21% among consumers, and this included likes, comments, and shares. This may not seem like a big percentage at first glance, but it was 54 times higher than the engagement which Pinterest received, and about 10 times higher than Facebook's engagement response. It was even 84 times higher than Twitter's engagement rate, so it is easy to see why Instagram has become a beloved social media tool when it comes to advertising products and services.

Let's take a look at some of the different types of advertising campaigns which are available to you.

Instagram Campaigns and the Options Available

Instagram has a couple of categories of campaigns for a brand to choose from. Each of these categories is aimed at reaching different goals and employs the use of different tactics to achieve these goals. Some examples of the different types of ad campaigns which your brand could choose to run on Instagram are as follows:

Brand Awareness Campaigns: These types of campaigns are useful if your brand is pushing to increase awareness and visibility among your audience. If you're a new up and coming brand especially, this is how you get yourself out there and get noticed by your customers. If you are running this type of campaign, what you're trying to focus on is to show what is distinctively different about your brand, what makes you interesting and why customers will love you. 80% of users on Instagram follow at least one brand on their platform, and 75% of users have been shown to take some form of action after viewing a brand's content or post. So, even if they don't buy from you immediately, the least they might do is follow you and keep tabs on your latest updates.

Campaign for a Cause: Audiences love to see that a brand is more than just focused on making sales and profits. They want to see that your brand cares about something other than its sales figures. Younger audiences especially, love to get behind a good cause, and a campaign that showcases your brand caring for a cause is a good way to shine the spotlight on your business. Your campaign for a cause should be a cause that your audiences will be able to relate to, something that resonates with them. For example, Dove launched their #DoveWithoutCruelty campaign, which emphasized the brand's commitment to not test its products on animals. Dove partnered with PETA and other social media influencers to promote this cause and it resonated well with a lot of other Instagrammers out there.

Contests Campaigns: This one needs no real introduction. You see them being run all the time by businesses both big and small across Instagram constantly. What makes them so effective is the simplicity of these campaigns. It usually doesn't take much for the audience to participate in these contests, and that's what they love about it. Your audience doesn't want anything that is too complicated or troublesome. They want ease, convenience, and excitement. Contests campaigns should be as simple as tag a friend for a chance to win or comment below for your chance at an awesome prize, perhaps even tag us in your best shot and you could be the lucky winner. This type of campaign should involve the audience in no more than two steps maximum, anything more than that and you run the risk of losing their interest.

Promotional and Sale Campaigns: Another frequent tactic which is often used by a lot of businesses are sale and promotional campaigns. This is another favorite which usually generates a lot of engagement because audiences are rewarded for their participation. This makes it worth their while and therefore, eager to participate. Especially when the steps are simple and straightforward. Like your contest campaigns, you want to keep your entry steps to no more than two at the most. Sale and promotional campaigns are perfect during the festive season, especially Christmas when consumers are likely to be in a more joyful mood and more willing to spend than they might be at any other time during the year. It is also great for running flash sales or one-time sale offers, where it prompts the audience to take some action because the special offers aren't going to last very long.

Product Launch Campaigns: This one is the perfect complement to a new product or service which your brand may be trying to launch. Product launch campaigns are the perfect tools to help build a buzz, create excitement and create anticipation about your upcoming launch. Especially among existing audiences and customers who already follow your brand on Instagram and love your business. When they see a new product launch campaign, they will be eagerly anticipating its release and more likely to engage even more with your brand because of it.

How to Set Up Successful Advertising Campaigns on Instagram

Having plenty of good ideas for your next Instagram ad campaign is a great place to start. What's even better though, is having a sound strategic plan behind those campaigns to ensure maximum success. A goal without a plan is a goal which is ineffective, so lay the foundation for your groundwork with the following tips to help you make the most out of your Instagram advertising campaigns:

SMART Goals Are Your New Best Friend: The letters in a SMART goal stand for Specific, Measurable, Attainable, Realistic and Time-Based. Every goal that you set should meet all these five criteria to optimize your ad campaign's potential. For every goal that you set, ask yourself if this is specific enough. Is the goal that you've set out measurable? Is it attainable and realistic enough to be attained and accurately measured? It is realistic budget-wise given your current resources? Is the duration of your campaign (time-based) enough to get you the results that you're hoping to achieve? When you first started your business, you had to draw up a detailed business plan which was going to guide you to what your next steps should be to get your business off the ground. Your SMART goals are now going to be your "business plan" for your advertising campaigns to help you achieve the results that you're after.

Planning Your Content: It is simply not enough to **want** to do a campaign. You need to plan your content down to the finest detail. SMART goals would come in handy in this instance because it helps you be definitive with the steps and the actions that you're taking. Having a marketing campaign is more than just trying to take some pretty pictures of interesting videos and including them into your campaign. The content must be carefully **planned and mapped out**, with a specific purpose and a reason behind each content. Every content in your campaign should be one that makes sense, and the content needs to be effective in building up excitement among your audience. If your campaign consists of a single post, that one post needs to be strong enough to draw them in and entice them to take action. If your campaign consists of a series of posts, it should be a series of visuals or videos that make sense, and when you put them all together, they should reveal the bigger picture. Campaigns are about building momentum, and there is a lot of work that needs to go into curating your content before it is ready to be part of your advertising campaign.

Utilizing Your Stories and Your News Feed Together: Avoid relying on just one method of approaching and reaching out to your audience. Make use of Instagram's multiple channels for an even more, power-packed outcome. Instagram is not just about the content that appears on your newsfeed, especially with the introduction of Stories and IGTV into the mix. 400 million Stories on Instagram are being watched daily, and this is where your business needs to be, utilizing the story ads for your best campaign yet.

Metrics Matter, So Track Them: Tracking your metrics is a must if you want to know you're on the right track to creating unstoppable Instagram campaigns. However, you want to specifically track the metrics which matter most. SMART goals again are going to prove to be very useful in this instance. Before you launch your campaign on Instagram, you're going to want to identify which key metrics you should be focusing on to begin with. This would depend on the type of campaign which you are running. There are various tools available to track your social media metrics, and some of these analytics tools are even unique and specific to Instagram. Establishing a baseline will help you accurately track and measure the impact that your campaign is having.

Setting the Right Budget: Possibly one of the most important factors which should not be overlooked. It'll be disappointing to spend all that time planning a fantastic campaign, only to realize that a lot of the things you want to do is going to fall outside your budget. Setting the right budget for your campaign will help you best identify that tactics which are going to be the best moves for your business, and which approach is going to make the most sense at this time. If only businesses could run on unlimited funds, there would be endless possibilities marketing-wise, but that's not always a reality. You can still create unstoppable marketing campaigns which become massively successful, you just need to plan a campaign that is going to match your budget.

Posting the Right Amount: You want your campaign to be a hit, which means that you're probably thinking it would be best if you posted as often as possible so audiences don't miss it. Well, it's a yes and no with this one. Posting frequently and remaining active is something that brand's need to do every day, but knowing how often you should be posting is the defining difference here. Studies have shown that the best engagement rates would fall between an average of one to two posts per day, while the time of day would depend on how often your target audience is active. Posting far too frequently, even during campaign periods, puts you at risk of "spamming" your audience's news feed, which could turn them off to your campaign entirely.

Chapter 5: Organic Traffic And Growing Your Page

Perhaps the essential part of being on Instagram is growing your following so that you can have an audience to market to. You have contributed to your ability to grow your following and increase your outreach. There are still several things that you can do to improve your Instagram account. Start seeing higher engagement rates. In this chapter, you are going to discover what it takes to grow your following and start generating success through your Instagram account.

Encouraging Engagement on Your Page

The first thing that you can do to start increasing your audience is to encourage people to engage with you on your page. Remember, the Instagram algorithm favors it when people engage on other users' pages, which means that if you can get your followers to start engaging with you, then that would be good. You can feel confident that they are going to start seeing more of your content, too. You can encourage engagement in two different ways: engaging with others and asking for engagement from your followers.

When you engage with the people who follow you regularly, they feel more inclined to engage with your posts because they begin to feel the development of a relationship. The back-and-forth support between you and your audience becomes a regular part of your relationship. When you go out of your way to go through your follower list and start engaging with people, you actually "break the ice" between yourself and them. This makes them feel more comfortable and engaged with you and your brand. You can do this by regularly going through your list of followers and tapping on random accounts and engaging with their content. Leaving a few heartfelt comments and liking some of their recent posts is an excellent opportunity to start engaging with people. This also inspires them to like back your content the next time they see your content. As you post, you can also ask for engagement by saying things like, "We love summer! Do you?" This encourages people to speak up. You can also increase engagement by writing captions that say things, like, "Comment with your favorite _____!" or "Tag a friend who would love this, too!"

Asking your followers to engage with your content in this way helps them break their thought process from mindless scrolling. Instead, you help them choose to participate in your content. Another great way to encourage engagement is to run giveaways on your page. This allows you to set rules that require individuals to engage with your post to enter the giveaway. Often, companies will decide on what they want to give away. Then they will set the requirements for individuals. For example, "Follow us, tag a friend, and share this post to your stories to enter in the giveaway!" Then, they will leave the giveaway for a certain period, allowing them to experience plenty of engagement from their followers. This type of behavior drives up engagement on that one post, but it will also support you in driving up engagement on the rest of your posts as well. You do not want to be engaging in too many giveaways, however. Two to four giveaways per year are plenty, and this is a great way to get involved with more followers.

Regularly Updating Your Following List

The people and the hashtags whom you follow are the ones that populate your main home screen, which allows you to see images that everyone you are following shares posts regularly. You want to ensure that you are regularly updating your following list so that you are only seeing people who reflect those that are actually associated with your branding or positioning. You might feel inspired to follow personal interests on Instagram, but this is typically best reserved for private personal accounts instead of business accounts. You want to ensure that your time spent scrolling through your followed accounts is spent investing in the growth of your business so that this becomes productive in the long run.

You can update your following list by going through the people you follow and unfollowing anyone who does not make sense to your brand. This way, you are not seeing content that is entirely irrelevant to you or following accounts that are unlikely to provide you with any return on your engagement. You can only support or unfollow up to 60 accounts in an hour, so take your time with this, and do it regularly so that you do not have many changes to make to your account. It would help if you were doing this every week so that you are staying relevant in your industry and seeing the latest trends and people who are coming up. Once you have unfollowed everyone who is not connected to you, you can start going to your most popular hashtags. See if there are any new hashtags or followers for you to pay attention to through the top posts in these searches. This way, you can start following new users who may support you in bringing more attention to your account each time you engage with their content or interact with them.

In addition, when you follow new hashtags that are trending in your niche, you can keep tabs on what's hot. You can also go ahead and start using those hashtags on your photographs so that you can stay relevant, as well. This type of research creates two powerful opportunities for growth in one move, so it is worthy of your regular attention and time!

Saying the Right Thing at the Right Time

On Instagram, you need to make sure that you are answering the right thing at the right time. By posting the right content at the right time, you can ensure that you stay relevant and that your content relates to what your audience is going through or thinking about. Your audience will be likely paying attention to and engaging with your content. The easiest way to say the right thing at the right time on Instagram is by following your audience.

Paying Attention to the Trends

Pay attention to the latest trends, concerns, and issues. That may be arising that people are paying attention to. For example, if you are in the blogging industry and you blog about current events concerning famous people, you would want to stay up-to-date on all of the latest trends and gossip. You would also want to blog about them as soon as they reach your eyes. The same would go for any industry that you are in. The moment you see a trend or topic waving through your industry, you need to be prepared to get on board with it, customize how you share it according to your unique brand, and offer it as soon as possible. In addition to following unexpected trends that arise in your industry, you also need to be following expected trends like holidays or scheduled events that are relevant to your audience. For example, if you are in the fashion industry, you should be paying attention to popular fashion events like

Fashion Week and the Victoria Secret Fashion Show. If you are in the tech industry, you should be paying attention to the latest device launches and information regarding events that are big in the tech industry, like the annual E3 event.

These types of events occur consistently, and they are extremely helpful in allowing you to stay relevant in your industry. Pay attention to the information being released by those who drive the industry like influencers and developers. It is important that you avoid talking about things out of season or out of turn, as sharing information too long after the event occurred can result in coming across as irrelevant or outdated. Typically, people who see companies sharing outdated information will believe that this company is not paying attention and does not care enough to stay in the loop with what is going on in their industry. As a result, people will not follow you. Remember, we live in the digital age where information can become available fast, and trends can rise and fall even more quickly. It would help if you were ready to get into these trends and start creating your brand's name in the heat of the moment, not after the trend or information has already started declining in popularity.

If you find that staying with the trends is harder than it looks, try finding three to four people or blogs. Follow those who are always quick to jump into new trends, and pay attention to these individuals or resources. This way, you are not overwhelming yourself by trying to follow too many people at once, becoming lost in what is relevant, what is a trend, and what is entirely irrelevant to you and your audience.

Targeting Your Audience Through Your Words

You now know that Instagram's biggest way to target audiences is through hashtags. This is how you can reach new audience members and start growing your audience fast. However, there is another verbal element that comes into play when it comes to creating an impact through your captions and writing. This is by having words in your captions that resonate with your audience.

You do not want to be using words that do not make sense to your audience or that sound completely irrelevant or outdated. This will lead to your audience becoming disinterested in reading what you have to say and struggling to actually "follow" what you are trying to tell them.

The best way to speak like your audience is to pay attention to what they care about by following them back and listening to how they are speaking. Regularly scroll through your feed and read what the people you follow are saying so that you can get a feel for what their language is like, how they tone their messages, and if there are any unique slang words, phrases, or acronyms that they are using to connect with their audiences. The more you read your niche's captions and comments, the more you are going to become familiar with how they are speaking, what they are saying, and what they are reading. This way, you can begin emulating their language through your posts and saying things in a way that makes sense to your audience.

When you do start emulating your audience, there are a few things that you will need to refrain from doing to avoid having your audience tune out from what you are saying. One thing to remember is that you need to prevent emulating your audience to the point that you lose your authenticity because you sound like you are identical to those whom they are already reading. Make sure that you pay attention to your brand's voice and your mission statement and adapt the industry's language to meet your tone and not the other way around. If your mood seems too off-base for your industry, you can consider casually adjusting it slightly to fit the industry's needs more. But do not begin changing your approach too frequently, or you will come across as fake and untrustworthy. The second thing that you need to avoid doing is creating messages that are filled with industry jargon that your general following is unlikely to understand.

If you attempt to use industry jargon that is commonly used between those who sell products and services in the industry, but that is unlikely to be recognizable by those who purchase in or follow the industry, you may lose your following solely because they do not understand you. You do not want to be creating gaps and confusion in your marketing by using language that your audience does not know because this can make it unnecessarily challenging for people to follow you and support your business. Keep it simple, speak in a way that your audience will understand, and adapt the industry language to suit your brand's message and purpose.

Leveraging Instagram Stories

Instagram Stories are a powerful tool that can be used not only to nurture your existing following but also to attract new followers for your business. When you use your Instagram stories correctly, you can create a significant influx of engagement from your followers and add a personal opportunity to connect with your brand. It also allows you to create a more interactive page overall. On Instagram, people love interacting with the brands that they love and consuming as much of their content as they can, and Instagram offers plenty of ways for followers to do just that. As you upload stories throughout the day, you create the opportunity for your followers to feel like you are genuinely thinking about them throughout the day, which establishes a connection of care and compassion between you and your followers. Not only will this help you maintain your existing followers, but it will also help new or potential followers see how interactive and intimate you are with your following, which leads to them wanting to be a part of your audience as well!

The reason that stories work is simple. People are nosy, and they like to know the insider's information. This is not a bad thing either, but rather just a simple human experience where we all desire to be a part of something bigger than ourselves. And we want to connect with those around us to become a part of that "something bigger." You can position yourself as the facilitator of that "something bigger" by turning your brand into an experience that people can enjoy and an entity that they can share an intimate and compassionate relationship with. Stories give you a great option to do that because every picture or short clip you share reflects a part of your personal behind-the-scenes experiences. You can also curate your story feed to offer an even more exclusive and intimate feel by purposefully sharing things that will allow others to feel like they are genuinely connected with you through your feed.

The key to making your stories intimate and leveraging them to attract new followers and maintain your existing ones is to make sure that the content you share in your stories is exclusive and unlike anything that you are sharing anywhere else. Be very intentional in sharing things that are more personal and "private" than what you would share on IGTV or on your feed itself because this way, people feel like they truly are getting that private insight into your brand. Instagram stories are already somewhat exclusive because, after 24 hours, they are gone and cannot be viewed again. You can play up that exclusivity thing by sharing the right content, mentioning things that you shared previously that new followers can no longer see, and even by suggesting outright that your story feed is exclusive. Say things like, "Keep your eyes on my stories because I will be announcing an exclusive offer here first... Get it three days earlier just by watching the story!" or something similar to this. Another way that you can leverage Instagram Stories is by making story highlights which can enable your new followers to see exclusive tidbits of your previous stories.

So, if you are someone who regularly travels, and you often share intimate travel experiences with people, such as the restaurants you dine at or the people you meet, you might consider sharing these in your stories. Then, you can create highlights of certain moments from your travels that were most exciting or interesting so that your new audience can glance back through your stories and start feeling more intimately connected with you right away. Leveraging your highlight reels in this way is a great opportunity to show your new followers what to expect, give them that feeling of having known you and your brand for a long time already, and increase their interest in you right from the start.

Using IGTV to Increase Your Following

IGTV is a great way to increase your following. These videos stay in place for as long as you leave them up, which means that followers can look back through your IGTV channel and watch stuff that you put up days, weeks, months, or even years ago once it has been around long enough. You can leverage IGTV to create new followers by creating excellent IGTV videos and then promoting them elsewhere on the net so that people are more likely to click over to your channel and watch. Once they see your video and the quality of the content you create, they can choose to follow your page to get more if they decide that they like you. The big opportunity with IGTV is that you can promote your IGTV channel just like you would a YouTube channel or any other free video content on the net.

By creating great content and then sharing it around the net, you can encourage individuals to go over to your Instagram to be able actually to see the video. This means that you can funnel people from Facebook, Twitter, Snapchat, email, and any other social media platform to Instagram so that they can catch your free content and learn from it. To make your content accessible, you need to make sure that the IGTV videos you make are worthy of receiving views. In other words, you need to create high-quality and engaging content. Your audience wants to pay attention so that when you share it with other platforms. They are more likely to click through your channel and watch the content that you created. The best way to create valuable content is to offer entertainment, insight, or guidance concerning your industry so that your audience is more likely to pay attention to it and watch it. For example, if you are an astrologer, you can create daily videos offering the astrological forecast for the day. If you are a sports announcer, you can create a daily video that highlights the most memorable sports moment of the week or the latest stats of famous players or teams based on the sport that you announce. If you are an educator of sorts, you can create a simple ten-minute or less tutorial on how your audience can do something for themselves that ties with your industry or your area of expertise.

By creating valuable content like this, you make it easier for your audience to understand why and how they are gaining value from your IGTV, which means that you will have an easier time promoting it and getting traction from that offer. Once you have created fantastic content, make sure that you leverage it in every way that you possibly can. Share it across all of your other social media platforms, talk about it in your stories, write about it in your latest post, and make sure that you save it for a future date. If you create timeless content, you can always use it as a reference to older videos when a few weeks or months have passed so that you can use them as a marketing opportunity all over again. For example, if you are a make-up artist and you did a specific tutorial, you can promote the video as soon as you make it, and then refer back to it if you notice someone famous wore a similar look in a recent event. This is an excellent opportunity to create one piece of content that has maximum impact, meaning that you can gain even more followers just from one excellent time investment. When it comes to marketing, that is really what it is all about!

Leveraging Influencers the Right Way

Brands and influencers go hand-in-hand, as they are both responsible for helping to generate success for the other. If you are not yet aware, influencers are individuals who build a trusted following in a particular industry and then advertise for industry-specific brands to their existing audience.

A great example of an influencer, or a family of influencers rather, would be the Kardashian-Jenner-West family, who is known for becoming and staying famous for the reason that most people cannot understand. This is because this particular family blew up around the same time that influencers were becoming a thing, and they leveraged their star power to begin making brand deals and endorsing companies. At this point, most individuals in the family have their businesses, although they still make money by supporting other products and marketing these products to their respective audiences. Influencers are solely focused on generating a massive following of people who like and trust them in a specific industry that interests them the most and then marketing to their audience for the products and companies that they want. As a brand, you can leverage influencers from your industry by having them test out your products or services and market them to their audience. Since their audience is already established and trusting in the influencer, you can trust that once the influencer has tried and endorsed your products, your recognition and sales will increase as well. The key here is making sure that you are working with influencers correctly. On Instagram, there is an unfortunate trend of companies that are attempting to work together with influencers and who are going about it in the wrong way, which results in losing a lot of money in this area of potential growth.

These companies, not knowing that they are making such drastic mistakes, find themselves attempting to work together with low-quality influencers or individuals who are not yet authentic influencers, which means they are not making a massive impact. Rather than having their products in the hands of people who can make a difference, they are attempting to get their products into the hands of people who do not, indeed, have an impact on their target audience. Typically, they will do so by encouraging potential "influencers" to buy their products and then make money anytime they purchase the products. In the end, the most significant way that the company is making money is by having the would-be influencers buying products and not by marketing the products to their target audience. When companies use this method, they end up looking spammy and careless, which results in them being seen as low-rate companies that are not worthy of being trusted or invested in. In the long run, this leads to an unsustainable practice, which can also lead to the premature demise of a company that could have otherwise succeeded in the online space. If you want to leverage influencers, you need to make sure that you are getting your products or services into the hands of people who can have an impact on your growth because they are already so connected with your target audience. Although you may lose some money by giving products away for free to these influencers, you will ultimately end up gaining cash because they will drive a lot of traffic to your page and your website. To create this positive and sufficient momentum in your business, you need to ensure that you are plugging into deals with the right influencers. Be very intentional and cautious about whom you offer your products or services to, and make sure that every single influencer you work together with can genuinely make a positive impact on your business.

Also, approach them professionally through their messages or email if they provide one and not through their comment's section on their photographs as this also comes across as unprofessional and spammy. If you want your company to look poised, respectful, and worthy of trusting and investing in, you need to make these long-term investments properly.

Increasing Your Posting Visibility

When you are posting on Instagram, you want to make sure that your posts are getting seen so that you can maximize your visibility, engagement, and traction overall. Instagram's algorithm favors individuals who get a lot of traction on their posts quickly and will ensure that even more people see these posts by placing it in more favorable viewing spots. If you want to gain these more favorable viewing spots, there are a few things that you can do to maximize your posting visibility and earn more followers overall. As you already know, a posting schedule is a valuable way to start increasing your posting visibility. It enables you to be put at the top of search feeds around the same time that your audience would be looking for your types of posts.

You can also ensure that you are engaging with other people before you post so that you appear higher in their newsfeed with your new posts as well. Another way that you can increase your posting visibility is by choosing hashtags that are only used 300,000 times or less overall, as these make it easier for you to be posted in the "top posts" section of the hashtag. Most people will browse these posts first, so being seen in this section ensures that you are going to be seen more frequently by people in your target audience. Another way that you can increase visibility is by creating high-quality posts and posting them consistently between one and three times per day. The more you post, the more you will be seen, and if your content quality is high, people are going to continue following you and paying attention to your page. When you post content, follow all of the strategies to ensure that you are creating content that people want to pay attention to and engage with. Never post a photograph that is too low in quality, as this will result in you having fewer followers or people unfollowing you because they may think that your standards are going down. You may notice that more significant influencers and brands do occasionally post lower quality photographs, and the reason is that they can get away with this easily. They have a huge following already, and they are unlikely to be impacted by one image. You, however, can be affected early on in a massive way. You want to avoid having people think that you are, in any way, posting low-quality content as this can lead to the loss of credibility and, eventually, followers. Lastly, if you want to maximize your visibility, make sure that you are engaging specifically with the people who are following you. These are the individuals who already see you in their newsfeeds, which means that they are the ones who will be most likely to engage with you quickly when you post new content. If you can get your real following to join soon, it will be easier for new followers to find you in their discover pages or on the top post tabs, which makes it more likely for you to be identified and followed by your target audience.

Engaging With Your Followers

This is a great way to maintain your existing following, but it is also a great way to discover new people who will want to follow you. Think of it this way. Your current following is already a part of your target audience, which means that they likely connect with people who are a part of your target audience by going to your followers' pages and connecting with them through their content. You establish a greater connection with your following, which is also increasing your ability to be found by their followers and friends. When their audience sees you commenting on their posts, if they are interested in what your brand has to offer, they may then click through your page and locate you. So, not only will this improve the way the algorithm works in your favor, but it will also add another avenue for people to discover you on Instagram. Another way that you can leverage your existing following to gain more followers is to go to your followers' pages and click onto pictures that are relevant to your industry. For example, if you sell bikes and your followers post an image of the mountain biking on a cross-country trail, this would be relevant to your industry. You can then look at the list of everyone who has liked this picture and begin engaging with these individuals by going to their pages, liking their content, commenting on a couple of images of theirs, and then following that individual.

This shows genuine interest, helps you stand out to that individual, and increases their chances of following you back. Of course, Instagram only allows 60 new follows or unfollows per hour, so make sure that you leverage this tool carefully to avoid being seen as spammy or overwhelming to the algorithm or your audience. Once these new individuals follow you, your process of going through your followers and engaging with their content will further support you in maintaining and building your following because it makes it clear that you care. If you engage with someone to earn their following and then never engage with them again, people will start to see your brand as superficial, which can lead them to unfollow you or no longer engage with your content. Keep yourself genuine and connected as much as you reasonably can so that you are always building better relationships with your existing audience and new relationships with your potential audience. Lastly, anytime your audience connects with you by commenting on your pictures, replying to your stories, or messaging you, make sure that you engage with that individual. This shows that you genuinely care about them and what they have to say, and it creates a positive relationship between you and that individual. Take some time out of your day each day to respond to all of these forms of engagement to make sure that you are investing in building a meaningful audience. On Instagram, which revolves around its social experience, a little bit of returned engagement can go a long way when it comes to building lifetime fans and relationships with your audience.

Analyzing Your Results to Increase Your Growth

Finally, you need to make sure that you are analyzing your results on Instagram to encourage higher growth on the platform! You can analyze your results either through the in-app analytics provided through Instagram itself or through a third-party application if you choose to use one of those. You can do this; however, you feel most confident, as long as you are regularly checking in to see how your content is performing. By periodically checking in, you can ensure that you can track trends in what your audience likes the most, what content gets the best engagement, and what earns the most likes on your page. As you monitor these trends, it becomes easier for you to understand what types of pictures, content, and offerings your audience likes the most, which means all you need to do is start creating more of that type of content for your page. Your analytics are not only going to support you in discovering what kind of content you need to be creating for your page, but it will also help you determine what you should be creating and offering more for your audience. These numbers will tell you exactly what products or services your audience enjoys the most and what they are buying the most, which allows you to begin offering the same types of products or services. If your business is solely on Instagram, you can create offerings that are specific to your Instagram audience and focus on expanding in the area that your Instagram audience seems to support. If your business exists on several platforms, then you can pay attention to your analytics across all platforms and incorporate this into all of your future offers.

If you find that the analytics vary from platform to platform, consider creating a variety of offers and then selling the offers that sell best on each platform exclusively on that platform. So, if you are a computer technician, and you find that Instagram users seem to be more interested in purchasing tech products and accessories from you and Facebook, individuals seem to be more interested in buying your actual services. You can market, respectively. Any time you have a new product available, emphasize your marketing around that product on Instagram and market only slightly on Facebook. Then, whenever you have a service to offer, place emphasis on your marketing for that new service on Facebook, and only refer to it a few times on Instagram. This way, both audiences know that there is more to your business than what you are sharing exclusively on that platform. Still, you are not bombarding either audience with content that they do not typically pay attention to.

The last part of your analytics that you need to pay attention to ensure efficient growth is how your audience on Instagram is relating to your actual target audience. On Instagram, a few accidental mistakes can lead to your audience being entirely off the target, which can lead to you having a tremendous following that is filled with people who are not interested in purchasing anything from you or your company. If you notice that your target audience and your Instagram audience are wholly misaligned or that your Instagram audience seems to engage with your content but never actually purchases anything, you need to start addressing your strategy. You want to make sure that you are putting your emphasis on the parts of your audience that are going to support your conversion ratios by becoming paying clients; otherwise, your time spent on Instagram will be pointless. If you do find that you do not have the impact that you desire, go back to the beginning of this book and start reviewing the chapters where we discuss carving out your niche and finding your audience on

Instagram. Refreshing yourself on this information and moving forward with a renewed perspective can support you and connect with the people that you mean to communicate with.

Chapter 6: You Must Follow These Laws For Writing Your Bio In Order To Instantly Generate Potential Buyers, Not Simply Followers

Instagram Bio – What Is it?

As already stated, your Instagram bio describes you as well as your business. When people visit your site, it is the first thing they lay eyes on. Every Instagram user has access to 150 characters for creating a bio. There is also the chance to use external links. Also, you can choose a username with up to 30 characters. Bearing this in mind, what should you achieve with your bio?

7 Things Your Instagram Bio Should Achieve for a Successfully Marketing Strategy

There are many things you should be able to achieve with your profile/bio. Because you have access to only a limited number of characters, this might seem like too much. Nevertheless, a good Instagram bio should take care of the following:

Make a means of contacting you available to Instagram users.

Show your uniqueness so your audience can have an understanding of the relevance of your brand.

Promote actions such as buying a product from your site, follow back, content sharing, etc.

Show your brand's personality. It should also ensure alignment between your website, other social media platforms, and your voice and style.

Display essential details about your business. This should include the sector your business is in.

The fantastic thing is there are lots of features you can take advantage of while putting up a bio. These many features make it easy to come up with a profile that will make it easy for users to have an understanding of your business and what services you offer.

Let's find out how to come up with an outstanding Instagram bio.

#1 Make Use of Keywords

"Name" is the first region you will notice as soon as you click on "Edit Profile". This should not be mistaken for your username. Your username is what other users will use to tag you, and is what will be displayed on your Instagram profile's URL. "Name" is the actual name of your page or business.

The first 30 characters you have access to while creating a bio consists of the area for your name. This can play a major role in promoting your Instagram SEO. When people run a search for anything on Instagram, an analysis is carried out on the words made use of in the "name" sector in a bid to find a fit. Knowing this, if you are interested in ranking well on Instagram SEO, you have to use keywords that are essential in your niche. Ensure they are a part of your "name" field.

#2 The Right Way to Write Your Bio

Your Instagram bio has a considerable impact on your audience. By just taking a look at your bio, visitors should have an understanding of what your brand is about, as well as its relevance. Your bio should also be able to attract followers, as well as end up in an action that will benefit your brand. This action could be making a purchase.

With the available 150 characters, you should be able to put in as much information as possible. This might not be so easy because of the limitation in the number of characters. For this reason, we will look into important details that should be a part of your bio:

Add Humor: It is important that you make use of your brand's voice. This way, you can be consistent on all social networks you are on. Also, it makes it easy for your audience to spot you in the crowd. In addition to making use of a voice, humor will be appealing to some.

Hobbies and Interests: If your brand depends on you as an individual, you have to build the right connection with your followers. It is okay to reveal some of your values, beliefs, and interests.

Skills and Experience: If your audience can have an idea of how skillful you are in your field; it will be a lot easier for them to trust you.

Particular Niche or Service: If your business falls into a specific industry, it is vital that your audience is aware of the industry your business is in. Also, if you have a reputation for making a particular service available, this should be clearly stated on your Instagram bio. This way, you can easily attract those who might require your service.

There are a couple of other things you can add to your Instagram bio to increase value:

#3 Make Use of Hashtags

Making a branded hashtag a part of your bio is an important technique you should use. This will build a community for your brand and will develop your post engagement. An example of this is Airbnb which effectively makes use of a branded hashtag as a part of its bio and also makes use of it in urging the creation of user-generated content.

Allowing your followers to share their content through your community by making use of your branded hashtag helps develop an Instagram page that is engaging. With this, you can promote your company effectively.

#4 Use Emojis

With emojis, you can make your profile have an attractive appearance and still stay unique. Also, with emojis, you do not get limited by the character counts that limit words. This way, it is possible to put up more details about your brand that would not be possible with the use of text alone.

The following tips can help you make use of emojis while creating a bio:

Make attempts at mixing up words with emojis.

All emojis added to your bio should have a relationship with what your brand is about and should augment your bio.

Make use of emojis in bringing attention to a vital point of your content. It is also okay to use them as bullet points to make texts easier to read.

It is not a very good idea to use emojis without accompanying them with some text. Doing this might make your audience confused and could be a waste of space.

It is essential that you are creative while using emojis. Experiment with different emojis to find the ones that are most applicable to your brand.

#5 Website URL: Adding a Link in Your Bio

With Instagram, you can only put up a single clickable link. This link comes just under your bio. A lot of Instagram users display the homepage of their website here. This is the way to go if you want to have more traffic on your business's site.

However, if there is a change in your business and Instagram goals with time, you should make a change to your URL link. This way, you can support your latest objective. It is okay to add a link to your most recent blog post, as well as a marketing campaign. You can choose from among a lot of options. Knowing this, make it a point to get the best out of your link.

#6 CTA or Call to Action

Your Instagram bio is a perfect place to put a call to action. Your audience should be aware of what you need them to do. If possible, you should let them know how you want them to carry it out. An example of this is asking them to connect with you on other social media platforms. If you have products, it is okay to ask them to make purchases. If your business has a physical office, its address can be made a part of your bio. It can also display your hours of operation.

#7 Select a Profile Picture

This ends the process of creating a bio and getting your Instagram profile ready to go. It is important that you make use of a catchy profile picture. One way to do this is by using the logo of your brand. This is even more critical if you are already using it on your website, as well as other social media platforms. Making use of a symbol that can be identified easily makes it easy for your followers to locate you wherever you and your business are on the web. It will also make more people aware of your brand. Ideally, Instagram brand bios are made up of a couple of components. You can be very creative when making use of these components. Experiment with lots of emojis, calls to action, and informative text. If you update your Instagram bio very frequently, you will become aware of what your followers respond to and what works for your brand. As soon as you make your bio what it needs to be, you will need to put in effort into creating your brand.

Chapter 7: How To Use Instagram With Your Direct Sales Business

Optimizing your Instagram channel for direct sales will lead to enormous rewards.

This chapter will cover how to use Instagram with your direct sales marketing business. The purpose of this chapter is to turn your Instagram account into an income opportunity. By ignoring the fundamentals of marketing on Instagram, you allow the competition to succeed.

Marketing on Instagram grows your website traffic and number of views per month. Yes, Instagram is just that powerful!

Below I give you the top tips for all affiliate marketers:

1. Tell people what to do

Nothing will grow your business faster than telling your audience what you want them to do. This is a Call to Action. It works, it is time-tested, and it is true. In the fast-paced world of social media, you must show your audience how you can help them.

Then you immediately tell them where to go for that help. In fact, your audience will appreciate the "straight to the point" tactic.

From our first-hand experience, Instagram is a unique social media channel in this respect. A typical person on Instagram will to look at a picture, check the description, and follow the call to action. Simple as that. To earn sales on Instagram you must give a call to action. When the call to action precedes the amazing offer you get more leads. Sounds amazing right? Well, guess what? It works.

There are many ways to entice your audience. It all begins with putting the right images and calls to action out there. This leads to tip #2.

2. Identify your audience's preference

Images that appeal to the customer's preference is the most important step for monetizing business on Instagram. Finding, targeting, and staying relevant to your audience is the critical factor. And whether you make the most income from this platform. Identifying your audience's preference is a huge topic. I have seen what happens when business owners post the wrong content to the desired audience. Let's just say it isn't pretty!

Luckily, you are reading this with some understanding of your audience's preferences. So this should be simple.

Take a look back through your Instagram feed and check out the popular posts. What has received comments, shares, and likes? Your audience will have the same tastes and preferences you do. Start each Instagram post with the question "Would this image pique my interest?" "Would I buy this?" If you answer yes, then you have found great content.

Consider going to your competitor's pages as well. Check out their popular posts and images. As you find images your niche audience is interacting with, make similar ones for your page. Once you've established your audience's preferences, it is time to move onto tip #3.

3. Identify the profit locations

Your monetization options on Instagram stay limited when you represent a direct sales company. Most direct sales companies do not allow their affiliates to take out advertising space. Read the fine print on your affiliate membership. Chances are good that paid advertising is not allowed.

So what are you supposed to do?

Do you remember tip #1? The call to action? Your affiliate situation demands that you use a powerful call to action to a profit location.

But wait. Do not post your affiliate link in this location, create an intriguing freebie instead. Your goal is to lead the audience to content. You can post this freebie link on Instagram and any social network. This link will collect email leads from people who want more information.

What is content? Content is information your niche audience wants. If you represent the make-up industry then maybe a freebie on how to contour is a good option. If you represent the health and wellness industry, then low-fat recipes would work.

The purpose of these profit locations is to take your Instagram audience and turn them into leads. Give a call to action to "Click the Link in the Profile" in the description. This is your profit location. Next, you move from the profit location to a sales funnel. Keep reading for tip #4.

4. Educate, give variety and repeat

After you have led your audience to the profit location you need to have a plan of action. Take the leads who wanted your freebie and turn them into a product sale. We suggest an approach that uses three different features.

Start with education.

A lead who wants your freebie is a "freebie-seeker'. Until you follow up with education about your valuable products they will never buy.

Give them the information they need and start building trust.

Give your leads variety.

A fundamental of bridging the lead into a sale is to have a multistep follow-up sequence in place. Create a marketing plan that incorporates email marketing, discounts, and valuable "how to" graphics. Think of infographics that teach them a new technique with your products. Variety also means including invitations to webinars or other live events hosted by you. This is the key to moving them through to the sale, what works for some people will not work for others. You must have enough variety to capture sales from many different personalities.

Repetition.

Humans need to hear the same message an average of 12 times before it finally kicks in. You may feel exhausted at repeating your information about your products over and over. Understandable. But you must realize that your customers did not hear you the first time. They have not heard you the second or third or fourth time!

Don't make the mistake of thinking your one "before and after" image on Instagram is going to get you a sale. The purpose of Instagram marketing leads the prospect into a sales environment. It is here where you talk to them over and over again. If your audience heard the sales pitch the first time, you would have already had thousands of sales.

Since that is not the case, then chances are, they have not heard your pitch. Take them off of the social media channel with a call to action. Direct them to a 'profit location'. Put in place a variable marketing campaign and talk to them again, and again, and again.

5 Analysis & optimization

Analysis & optimization must be a large part of your Instagram strategy. There are two different analysis techniques you need to understand. Quantitative (measurement) and Qualitative (non-measurement).

Quantitative

Here is where you can measure the engagement with each image/post. Create (or use an analysis app) where you can calculate the interaction from each post. Your desired measurement is going to be the number of clicks to your link in profile.

You will want to measure how many of those clicks converted to a lead (they gave you an email). Quantitative measurement shows you revenue potential. When each of those leads follows your marketing campaign (tip #4) you have a good starting point.

Your goal is to make effective Instagram campaigns. So the more data you can add to this analysis, the more effective you'll be.

Day/time of day posted

Content type - link, photo, video etc.

Ratio of link clicks to lead captures.

Use this strategy to build a picture of which efforts are profitable, and which are a waste of time.

Qualitative

Qualitative analysis is looking at the aspects of your marketing that is not numbers. Your qualitative analysis will cover the aesthetics of your business. Here are some questions to get started with.

Am I providing enough information? Does my content support my efforts (giving people enough call's to action)?

Does my freebie link work well for the Instagram platform?

Given all that I know about marketing, do I come across as a "spammer"?

Am I offering true value to my target audience?

These qualitative measurements should be one of the most important considerations. Are you paying enough attention to the service that you offer or are you just trying to make a buck? Believe us. People know the difference between a salesperson and someone who leads with value.

The only way you will make sales is by being the value leader first through qualitative analysis. The more value you give away the more success you will experience.

This process is a long one. It may feel safe to aggressively promote your direct sales products on social media. Again, trust us. Take the time to represent yourself as the value leader and you will earn greater profit in the long run.

You have read 5 tips to monetize your direct sales business using Instagram.

1. Tell people what to do

2. Identify your audience's preferences

3. Identify the profit location

4. Educate, variety, and repetition

HOW TO USE INSTAGRAM EFFECTIVELY

Instagram is currently used by millions of people worldwide, and for a good reason: taking pictures and sharing them with your friends has never been easier! However, Instagram can be used in a very effective manner, not only for networking but for marketing purposes as well. If you have a business and you would like to promote it in the online environment, then this can be a great promotion tool. Having said that, here are 5 of the best ways to effectively use Instagram:

1. Hashtags can work like magic!

Twitter uses them, Instagram uses them and recently, Facebook has implemented hashtags as well. As a matter of fact, Instagram users interact mainly via hashtags, this is why you need to learn how to use them in your best interest. This aspect can be particularly useful for businesses who are looking for followers, as it allows them to make their content searchable and it will also trigger a viral effect that will benefit the business in the long run.

2. Photos and videos can tell a story

A photo can be worth a thousand words, and everybody knows that. Instagram is all about photos, but taking random photos will not take you very far, especially if you plan to use Instagram mainly for marketing purposes. One of the best, fastest and easiest ways to increase brand awareness and to boost sales is to post pictures of your product on a constant basis: they do not even have to be professional, they just need to highlight the main features and functions of the product in question and to appeal to the wide audience.

Same goes for videos: You can share videos with your employees in action, or you can make live product reviews. Regardless of your choice, videos and pictures are very likely to go viral, as people love media files more than text and they are likely to remember them over the years. If you own a new business and you want to make a name for yourself, then pictures and videos will surely come in handy!

3. Contests

People love freebies, discounts and all sorts of promotional offers, this is why you can never go wrong with a contest. A contest is a win-win: your customers will get a free product or service, while you get the chance to increase brand recognition. One great way to use Instagram for contests is to encourage people to share their own pictures of your product, and to reward the most suggestive or original picture. At the same time, you can use various tools that allow you to easily embed an Instagram feed or a hashtag feed into your website.

4. Keep track of your success

Tracking the success of your Instagram marketing campaign is essential. Fortunately, there are many comprehensive and user-friendly applications that allow you to track the customer growth, to see which are your most popular posts, to determine when the right time to post content and so on is. As irrelevant as these details may seem, at first sight, they can actually make a difference.

5. Connect with your user

Keeping in touch with your customers is important, especially for small and medium enterprises who have a limited target market. You can show your customers that you care about their feedback by simply replying to their comments or questions.

This will not only attract user-generated content, but it will also improve credibility and increase the visibility of your business. Do not underestimate the power of your Instagram followers, as they can contribute to the success of your business!

To sum it up, these are five of the best ways to effectively use Instagram to increase sales, boost the revenue and improve brand awareness.

HOW TO MARKET YOUR BUSINESS ON INSTAGRAM

Businesses using Instagram to promote their products, services and offers now have an even greater opportunity to market their wares to a super targeted audience. With the backing of Facebook, Instagram has recently launched its advertising platform that integrates with Facebook's amazing targeting capabilities and businesses are taking full advantage. Businesses know that users are watching their news feed. As a result, Instagrammers are 2.5 times more likely to click on newsfeed ads than ads on any other social media platform. So running Instagram ads for your business open up a world of opportunity.

Mobile advertising has surpassed newspaper advertising for the first time in history and large and small businesses alike are achieving measurable results with social media advertising. Instagram advertising has already generated more than half a billion in revenue and is projected to double within a year, which is proof that many business owners are putting their money where their mouth is.

More importantly, Instagram's ad platform is easy to use, it's fun and bubbling over with passionate and enthusiastic users. It has excellent metrics and is still affordable for small businesses. If you are already advertising your product with social media ads or trying to build your list then integrating Instagram ads into your marketing mix is essential.

Here are five tips to consider before running an ad on Instagram to grow your business brand reach, engage your followers, or attract your target audience to your offer.

1. Get the basics right. Make sure to fill out your business profile and bio on your business Instagram account. Make sure to use a clear, crisp version of your company logo as your profile picture.

2. Tell users WHY you are on Instagram. Since this is your business account, keep it business, not personal. Help users identify with your brand and just make sure not to be too sales.

3. Start with a plan. Strategize your Instagram (and all your social media) promotions by planning them out. Create a calendar for implementation that leads to your goal. Not having a plan is the main reason why businesses fail on social media, so do this before you start posting randomly or paying for traffic!

4. Don't let your hashtags be your voice. Instead, lend your business voice to your hashtags. Customize hashtags for branding purposes and for everyday posting, keep them relevant and searchable. It's great to use hashtags, just make sure to not lose control and generate too many in one post - deliver quality over quantity.

5. Upgrade your look. Images are everything on Instagram so make sure your images and video look GREAT. Savvy Instagram users want to see "beautiful" or read "funny" or relate to something meaningful. Use apps and other image/video tools to upgrade the look and feel of everything you post on Instagram.

Those are just a few tips to consider when using Instagram to market your business online. If you need more ideas about how to add your own flair to your Instagram posts without having to be a designer or photographer.

Chapter 8: The Pros And Cons Of Internet Marketing

Social media has been criticized from day one of its existence and there are certainly some downsides that come with it. That's not the question that you should be worrying about, though. With every negative there comes the opportunity for growth and development, so while the list below may be considered as cons or negatives in the eyes of some, it might be of little concern to others.

Internet marketing definitely has its pros and cons, and depending on how you look at it, some issues can be representative of both sides. Social media is constantly running, and this gives people the prime opportunity to make the internet work for them. There are ways to work around and overcome each problem with positivity and make it work for you as you develop your business strategy. However, you still have to be prepared to deal with the issues as they arise, and any negative effects that online marketing could bring your company.

Online marketing and sales go hand in hand in the social media world. Marketing strategies are put to the test as they display advertisements in different places on customers news feeds, along with posting sales and promotion tactics to their company's social media pages, as well. People don't tend to notice that they are being sold something when they look at fun advertisements and see people like celebrities or other key influencers holding a product or using certain items in videos. In the subconscious mind, it does take root and can be effective as far as sales go, but it's hard to produce concrete results when social media sales aren't recorded in any concrete way.

The Pros and Cons

Let's start with the pros of social media marketing. The number one pro across most business boards is that social media marketing is effective and cost-efficient. Companies don't have to spend a fortune on advertisements anymore because social media is allowing them to put out constant messages and giving them the ability to regularly interact with customers. Almost all social media websites are free to join. While there may be a small fee for the business accounts, they do include more resources to help businesses track customer interactions and trends on their homepages. Social media marketing could potentially cost anywhere from $4,000 to $7,000 a month. This may seem like a lot of money for such small posts, but compared to the cost of traditional marketing and the time spent on physical marketing materials, the benefits of social media marketing greatly outweigh that cost. When you take that into consideration, this means that the big businesses that are paying people to produce social media advertisements are still saving a substantial amount of money by advertising online rather than in print or on television. Any way a company can save money on marketing will always be considered a pro in the business world.

The next pro on the list is the reach of the audience. Social media markets are constantly expanding, and every time someone follows a new account or adds a friend online, a new branch is created on the internet. The reach of social media is more than most people might realize. Instagram has 77.6 million users and is constantly growing. As the reach continues to grow, it becomes possible for people to share posts from the website via text messages, emails, or even direct messages on the app itself. The reach of marketing is endless if you utilize the right people to help you spread your message.

Social media is instant. With the advent of social media, people no longer have to wait for companies to mail out press releases or send out mass emails. One post can be shared with millions within seconds and will stay posted on the company page for all to see if they need to refer to it or find it again. The ability to communicate with customers and followers has allowed businesses to become more personable and customer service oriented than they were before. Communication channels are more open and the ability to answer the questions and concerns of multiple people at once has become easier than ever. It also serves to create a direct, two-way interaction between businesses and people. There isn't a huge divide between big business and the customer now as more businesses are responding directly to customers on their social media pages and creating more brand loyalty by interacting with their followers.

Social media has made research and feedback easy. Social media is a business that is always open, which means that you can get instant feedback on your marketing campaigns. This allows you to update and fix any small problems with your products or services from the feedback that you are getting from people. You might not like all of the feedback from customers, but it will be beneficial in the long run. You are able to reevaluate and update your campaign if something isn't working. Social media has an edit feature, which you don't have when you put something into physical print. And yes, people have already seen the post, but that doesn't mean you can't make some changes and send it out again. While some may consider this a pro, it can also be a con. Feedback is instant, and while you hope for entirely good feedback, it won't all be. There will always be someone that has a problem with your company and wants to complain about it on a public forum. That is just the way of the world. Some people are never satisfied. It is important to note, though, that even negative comments can be used to your advantage online. You may not have come up with a perfect solution for the individual who originally posted, but the effort that you put in will still be displayed, and other customers and reviewers will notice the time and effort that was taken to resolve the situation. Feedback is important to customers because it gives them a better sense of the company's intentions when they release new products to market. Are they just trying to sell another product, or are they listening to what we have been saying? Will the issues from the previous versions be fixed with this new release? The reason that we see constant updates and improvements of products and applications is because of the reviewers and testers that let the company know that something isn't working. It's more than likely that you have seen a mobile phone game advertised on Instagram at some point or another. If you take a moment to scroll through the comments on that feed, you might notice a lot of complaints about bugs in the system or people commenting about the level that they reached and the excitement that the game brings them. While the game producer may reply to some of the positive posts, they are paying close attention to the negative ones and the comments that get likes on them, symbolizing that others agree with that statement. It creates a way for the company to get the feedback needed in order to improve their product and keep people involved with it.

The last pro may be one of the biggest and most important. Social media is easily tracked. There are loads of software and analytic systems out there that can show you when your customers are online and what they are looking at more frequently. It gives you a better understanding of what posts they like the most, and which ones could use some improvement. It also lets you set a schedule of when to post in order to reach more people at the most active times.

Then, there are the cons.

Perhaps social media's largest con is that it's time-consuming. **Very** time-consuming. There are programs out there that you can use to schedule posts and plan in advance, but there is no way to schedule customer interaction. The internet is 24/7 and someone is always awake. While neither you nor your company need to be awake all day or night, there needs to be someone prepared to handle the havoc in the morning. Like we mentioned earlier, feedback is immediate, and while some people won't see them right away, comments that are left on posts need to be addressed, especially if they are shining a negative light on the product. Someone needs to manually sift through the comments, watch what people are posting, and tag the company in in order to deal with any customer service issues that may arise. This also shows customer interaction in general. Having a social media team is essential to the success of posting online. It is best to have one person to post and one to respond at minimum to make sure the bases are getting covered.

The next con on the list is negativity. While this may seem obvious, people on social media can be very hateful. There is no way to filter out hate comments or liars, and they just have to be addressed quickly and properly. The biggest lesson to know before entering the social media world is that, no matter how much customer service you provide, there will always be someone who reacts negatively. It's especially easy for people to be negative online because they aren't dealing with you face to face. Every company typically has a way to deal with negative users and try to resolve problems for them, but you can't expect everyone to be pleased with the results. Eventually, you have to move on towards other solutions.

This con can also be considered a pro depending on how you look at it. Social media is constantly changing. On the downside, about the time you get comfortable with the way something is performing and being used, it's going to change. Like everything else on the Internet, social media evolves as everyone's needs change. The positive side is that, as it changes, you can change with it. The basics of internet marketing are still going to apply with whatever changes are made.

The next big con on the list is that whatever is posted on the Internet stays there. While, you can make changes and updates to your posts online, you cannot stop people from sharing, screenshotting, commenting on, and reposting your original message. Before you post anything to your page, make sure that it is ready to be sent into the online world.

With posts being more casual and easily posted online, it can be hard to keep up with the constant conversations that are taking place. You don't want to leave one of your posts up to the interpretation of others, which is why you need to be clear and concise with anything you share online. Read it and re-read it, and even have a co-worker or two read it before you publish it. This will save you some time and hassle of having to try and fix any mistakes.

Now, let's discuss ROI (Return on Investment). ROI is difficult to measure.

If you are given the right tools to analyze ROI you should be able to measure it effectively as it relates to social media. You can then tell what is working and what isn't in order to improve your sales and link them back to the online platform. Businesses have social media platforms designed to track people's actions on their page but the problem with this is that it isn't always exact when it comes to sales, and it can't always be proven. If someone sees your Instagram post about the 20%

off sale happening from Friday through Monday, but you also have that same message posted on your website and in an email that was sent out to all previous purchasers, there is no exact way to tell where that shopper came from. You could utilize an optional survey at the end of a purchase, or use promo codes to try and track where people saw the information. Otherwise, it will be a difficult measurement to get.

Is It Worth It?

The short answer is a resounding yes! There is no world in the future where Internet marketing and social media platforms will fail. While it is true that different platforms may come and go, their evolution will remain the same. Adaptation to new programs and settings may take some getting used to, but so does every new business marketing strategy out there. If your company is trying to get away with not building its social media presence, then you should deeply reconsider this. The rise of social media isn't going to be a passing trend, and with more and more people turning to Instagram and LinkedIn for connections in both the business and personal world, sales and marketing need to follow suit.

There are pros and cons to having a social media account, and there are a hundred different factors that can affect each one, but social media and Internet marketing are only going to grow as we move into the coming years. When you look at the big picture as far as marketing and sales go, Instagram has helped create more profit for businesses. Social media has created a gateway between customers and businesses where communication is key. People like interacting with other people. Seeing responses and hearing from businesses as they address problems will make customers feel more comfortable buying from them and returning to make more purchases.

The end goal of marketing online is to have customers return to your business and have them promote your company by word of mouth. They may be actually talking about the company or spreading the news online. You want customers to be excited to share your products with their social media family and to spread the word of their experience with your business. As discussed earlier in the book, brand advocates are on your side. Having people who speak on behalf of your company online is the goal. If you can get to the point where you have brand advocates and ambassadors sharing your product, then you will see online results. It won't be immediate and it will be time-consuming, but your company will be able to build its online brand and create a reputation for itself on social media.

Building a following, getting people to share pictures of their products, and discovering what's trending are all tasks that need to be worked on and accomplished every day for the social media team. There needs to be dedicated response times for customers and times where promotions are being put out. There are also a lot of little steps in between that have to be handled as well. While social media is difficult, especially when you are trying to work and manage multiple platforms at the same time, it's going to be the future of all marketing. Slowly, all print will fade and online shopping will become the majority of where sales develop. Be ready to accept the change of social media development. Learn how to improve your online business as you market to different crowds and people around the world.

Chapter 9: How To Create A Brand Story With Instagram

Now that you understand your brand voice and also your ideal customer, it's time to get around to creating that brand story. You want your brand story to be as unique as the story of a person. No two people are exactly alike, are they? Neither should two Instagram feeds!

Even if you are selling the exact same product or service as a competitor, it's your brand story that will differentiate you and help you attract the following you need to be an Instagram success. Doing this will require a concretely planned approach to your feed.

When somebody opens up your Instagram feed, they should see coherent parts to a whole. This is why it's a bad idea to pepper your feed with random cat photos if your product or service has nothing to do with pets. Your story should make sense, and it should make sense at a glance.

Again, you want to avoid falling into the "catalog" trap where your Instagram feed reads like a product listing. Your brand isn't only your product or service.

"Brand story" photos can include things like lifestyle photos - so long as those photos make sense with your story. For instance, perhaps simply posting pictures of cats would not be a good choice for Bob's Widgets, but if there happens to be a picture of a cat playing with a widget, that would be a good way to integrate Fluffy into the Instagram feed. Everything should be relevant to your brand and your company somehow.

In fact, involving pictures of Fluffy in with your brand story is absolutely vital, as it plays into how important it is for your Instagram brand to be unique. A picture of a widget has no personality - it is simply an object. A picture of a widget being batted around by a cute cat has tons of personality. Plus, then you can involve cat-related hashtags into that picture and give it even more exposure. Even people who aren't interested at all in widgets are interested in cats; this will give your feed more momentum.

So when you have your brand voice, use it to help create your brand story. You have the personality of your brand… how would your brand showcase that personality?

Chapter 10: How To Make Money Using Instagram.

Instagram is a platform for sharing your passion using short videos and pictures. It also allows you to connect with individuals who share similar interests with you, develop loyal followers, and become a top influencer in your specified niche. Now, lots of accounts on Instagram have tons of followers.

Typically, many brands have noticed the room for advertising the influence and reach of these accounts can create. For this reason, users with a decent amount of followers now have numerous ways to make money using the platform.

 What Do You Need to Earn Cash Via Instagram?

The leverage of an Instagram user stems from the numbers of followers he/she has. The reason is that Instagram profiles that have numerous followers offer connection to a massive market. If you are serious about earning money on Instagram, you need to begin small and take all the chances possible to enhance the follower count on your account. Now, let's go into this a little further.

Influence and Reach

The natural growth of your followers has a direct relationship with the level of reach your posts have. You have numerous options to expand your posts reach, but one that is important for making cash off Instagram are authentic and original posts. You will need to have no less than three thousand followers on your profile before it becomes lucrative. This means you need to invest the time to amass followers who find you trustworthy, and who believe your posts have something significant to offer them.

If you aim to use your Instagram profile in promoting the products and services of organizations, then you need more than good reach. This is because people still have to make a move and buy the product or service you are promoting. The capacity to coax your followers into purchasing the products or services you are providing is known as influence, and if you plan on becoming a leading influencer on Instagram, you have to learn the skill of persuasion.

Engaged Followers

If you are not getting comments or likes from those who follow your page, then it means your posts are not significant enough to keep them engaged and trigger a response from them. In contrast to this, if your posts are drawing in lots of likes and comments, it means the posts are helping your Instagram followers solve a specific issue they may be facing.

Also, the number of messages your Instagram followers send to you is something you should consider in determining how engaged your followers are with your posts and pages. For this reason, it is crucial that you have people continuously leaving comments on your posts, sharing them, liking them, and tagging their followers in your posts, if you are serious about sparking interest in profiles and brands that can help you make money on Instagram.

Ways to Earn Money on Instagram

There are numerous ways of earning cash available at your disposal. Below are a few of the top options:

Become an Influencer

Like we have covered above, being an influencer means you can influence your followers, and control the way they feel about products and trends. This will be due to your position and the trust you have developed with your online image.

You can choose to partner with organizations as an influencer, to promote the services and products they offer. Lots of brands are eager to work with influencers to advertise their services and products. This is typically done via sponsored posts because of the numerous benefits of advertising on Instagram offers.

Use Instagram to Sell Your Photos

This one is one that may seem obvious, but it can be a great way for photographers to showcase some of the work that you do. If you are an amateur or professional photographer, you will find that Instagram is the perfect way to advertise and even sell your shots. You can choose to sell your services to big agencies or even to individuals who may need the pictures for their websites or other needs.

If you are posting some of the pictures that you want to sell on your profile, make sure that each of them has a watermark on them. This makes it hard for customers to take the pictures without paying you first. You can also use captions to help list out the details of selling those pictures so there isn't any confusion coming up with it at all.

To make this one work, take the time to keep your presence on Instagram active. This ensures that the right people and the right accounts are following. This is also a good place to put in the right hashtags so that people are able to find your shots. You may even want to take the time to get some engagement and conversations started with big agencies in the photography world who can help you grow even more.

147

Become an Affiliate Marketer

Affiliate marketing shares some similarities with influencer marketing, but then there is a major difference; affiliate marketers lay emphasis on making actual sales for a commission on every sale as opposed to Influencers that help in creating awareness about a brand or product. This means if you choose to become an affiliate marketer, you are offered a commission for each product you sell.

When you want to work with affiliate marketing with Instagram, you need to post attractive images of the products you choose and try to drive sales through the affiliate URL. You will get this affiliate link through the company you choose to advertise with. Just make sure that you are going with an affiliate that offers high-quality products so you don't send your followers substandard products. And check that you will actually earn a decent commission on each one.

Being an affiliate is very simple. First, you get a unique URL, which is utilized by the affiliate program in tracking the number of individuals who click on the link and make a purchase from the website. This is the way you attain your commission. These promo codes or links take users directly to the page for purchasing the product. However, Instagram does not support the placing of clickable links in any location apart from your bio, which makes it challenging to use links. For this reason, Promo codes are the best routes for affiliates as you can integrate them into your Instagram stories and posts. With this, prospective customers will only have to input your promo code when they are about checking out, for you to attain your commission, while a discount is also offered to the customer on the product.

Trade Your Instagram Account

Many individuals deal in exchanging Instagram accounts for funds. This may be because they no longer have an interest in using Instagram for that moment, or they have a lot of accounts with decent follower counts and are interested in making cash.

Platforms like VIRAL ACCOUNTS and FAME SWAP are popular places to sell your Instagram accounts. Depending on the platform you choose to go with, the rates may differ, and you can do your research to find the price suitable for you and dispose of your account for a reasonable sum of cash. However, you need to think critically about this, because you never can tell when your account may be of use to you later. Before you sell-off, your account, make sure your mind has been made up.

Sell Products on Instagram

It is possible to use your Instagram profile to sell products, be it an online service, or a digital or physical product. If you have good reach on your account and you have developed awareness for the product, all that is left is for you to promote your company and watch people troop in to buy your goods or services.

Instagram has offered a very budget-friendly and easy means to buy and sell, and using this factor is quite easy. All you need to do is establish a great brand name, and when you have developed a specific level of trust, people may even begin to do your marketing for you.

A lot of entrepreneurs began their businesses from Instagram, and many of them are at the top of their fields and enjoying a continuous influx of revenue. The great news is that; there is enough space for everyone to benefit from this as well. So if you have a product to sell, Instagram may be an excellent platform to start.

 Get More Website Traffic Using Instagram

If you run a business which has a website, Instagram can offer a great platform to market that business. Raise awareness for your business and upload amazing images and content that can provide your business a distinct identity, then utilize than in drawing in visitors to your site.

If your audience finds your content engaging and relevant, they will want to learn more about your organization. To make this work, you need to add a link to your website on your bio, and visitors will be directed to your website from there. In turn, this will aid in increasing your product and service awareness, and with time, your conversion.

Drop shipping to Users on Instagram

As a drop shipper, it means you run a business without the need for a physical store. All you require is a dealer who can convey your merchandise straight from their storeroom to your clients, which eradicates having to hold expensive product inventory. You also don't have to deal with the process of shipping, and you function as your own agent.

The concept is similar to selling products; however, in this situation, you don't have to store any product of goods, which makes it seamless for entrepreneurs and owners of businesses.

There are numerous e-commerce channels like the well-recognized ones like OBERLO and SHOPIFY, which allow you to start a drop shipping store. To begin, you have to spot an ideal niche, then try out the product market to help you determine what would sell better. If you are looking for a cheap way of becoming a business owner, then drop shipping is a fantastic option, as it doesn't require a massive sum of cash to begin selling. If you use drop shipping the right way on Instagram, there is a possibility of earning a lot of money in the long run.

Create a Sponsored Post

Instagram users that have a following that is pretty engaged have the ability to earn some money through the platform simply by creating sponsored content that is original and that various brands can use. To keep it simple, a piece of sponsored product through Instagram could be a video or a picture that is going to highlight a brand or a specific product. These posts are then going to have captions that include links, @mentions, and branded hashtags.

Sell Advertising Space on Your Page

If you have a large enough following, you may be able to get other brands and companies interested in buying advertising on your profile. They will use this as a way to gain access to your followers in order to increase their own followers, sell a product, or increase their own brand awareness. This is the perfect opportunity for you to make some money from all the hard work that you have done for your own page.

There are many different ways that you can do this. You can offer to let them do a video and then post it as your story, promote a post on your profile, or use any of the other ad options that we discussed above. You can then charge for the type of space they decide to use, the amount of time they want to advertise for, and how big of an audience you are promoting them in front of.

Become a Brand Ambassador

This is something that is becoming really popular with MLM companies. There is so much competition on Twitter and Facebook that many are turning to use Instagram as a new way to promote their products and get followers that they may not be able to find through other means. And because of the visual aspects of the platform, these ambassadors can really showcase some of the products through pictures and videos.

There are many companies that you can choose from when it comes to being a brand ambassador. Since you have already taken some time to build up your audience and you have a good following, so if you can find a good product to advertise to your followers, you can make a good amount of money. You have to pick out a product that your followers will enjoy, ones that go with the theme of your profile to enhance your potential profits.

Chapter 11: Converting Your Followers To Clients

Your followers don't want more information. They already have as much as they can get. All they are interested in is the outcome the information will bring. They need to be sure that what you are offering them has a transformative value. You have a purpose. Your primary goal is to help those that need your products, services, or program. When they are happy and satisfied with your brand, you can drive sales and make profits. If you don't put in action and put yourself out there for your audience, this won't happen. Don't focus all your attention to growing your followers without focusing on how to turn these followers into clients.

At this point, you have gotten quite a reasonable amount of followers, so now you have to convince these followers that you are credible and worth doing business with.

The first step that will make a follower to skip other brands offering the same services or products you offer, and meet you for business, is by being different. You need to be different and act different from others. You don't need to look, sound, or appear the same way others do. You can still carve out a sub niche for yourself in whatever niche you are in even if it's populated. You should have an impact on your clients so they won't even notice you have competitors.

Your marketing style should be totally different from others. When you are unique and different, you won't be bothered about the price you set. Your clients will buy your services and products at whatever price you set because what you have to offer isn't a commodity.

Now you know the secret is being different and standing out from the crowd. I will guide you on how to stand out from the rest and use this advantage, leveraging on it to generate more revenue.

Have a call-to-action bio that adds value

This is where you get a chance to create a first impression with your client. Go straight to the point and tell your prospects why they need to do business with you. Tell them how your products or services will benefit and add value to them. You can offer them a lead magnet at this point. People love to get freebies a lot. In the long run, this will help in building your relationship with them. Let them know what they stand to gain and how you will solve their problems, if they choose to trust you.

Offer value in your posts

As addressed earlier, the key is being unique, so at this point you have to think up an idea that will set you apart from others in the same niche with you. When you have come up with the idea, focus on it. Make sure the posts you make align with this unique selling proposition.

Talk to your followers

Humans love to talk and communicate, and we are going to leverage on it. Involve your audience and strike up conversions with them. Make conversations to center around your unique idea. Ask them questions and engage them. Let them know you are open to building relationships and trust not just selling to them. When you ask questions, they tend to engage more with you.

Be unique and original

Most people cloak and cover themselves with masks. It is exhausting and at a point you won't be able to keep up. It will also prevent you from developing real relationships. Show your real self to your audience and quit pretending to be someone else. Even popular brands have die-hard fans and detractors. Your right audience will be able to relate better with you. Your Instagram life shouldn't be different from your offline life. Your audience will relate and trust you better if they believe you are real. If you don't mind, you can let your followers in on your life and who you are. If the service you are offering has impacted your life, share your journey with them. Remember, people do business with brands they know and trust.

Focus   on transformation value

Most of the other brands in your niche will focus on how great and wonderful their products, programs, and services are. But you are smarter and have gotten equipped to soar. You will have to focus on the benefits you have to offer. The focus should be placed solely on how these benefits will impact and make their lives better. You have to also focus on how your business will bring them comfort, peace, and solutions to the problems they are facing. This will not just generate sales for you, it will also place you as an authority in your niche. Converting your followers into customers can be easy and fast if you can simply focus and pay attention more to the reason why they should take action.

Instagram analytics

In every business strategy, there should be records for you to backtrack to. This is to ensure you are making progress, this is where Instagram Analytics comes into play.

Instagram analytics involves checking out the photo, video, or story that performed best and worst. This is done by tracking the key metrics over time. They can also be used to find out how photos of products performed against each other. You can do this by comparing the engagement data of each product photo against the other. Definitely, people are more interested in the product that has more likes, clicks, and comments. ,

Checking your Instagram analytics helps know what your clients are interested in and want. It also helps you to improve your content so your audience can get value from it and for you to drive more sales and traffic. Let's talk about some of the metrics you should be keeping track of:

Impressions

Impression is simply the number of times your video, story, or photo gets viewed. It also includes the number of users that while scrolling by in their feed, click and go through your page to look at a photo or go through your content. In other words, it refers to the number of views your photo or profile received.

Reach

It shows the total number of views too but in a more specific way. Reach calculates its own total number of views by the number of unique user views instead of just the number of eyes on it. In other words, it is how many people saw your post, photo or profile, and not just the number of views.

Engagement

It involves the total number of accounts that have made comments, liked, and saved a photo or video on your page. It doesn't count different comments from the same user in the same post.

The engagement rate is the percentage of followers that get engaged when you make posts. In order to calculate your average engagement rate, you have to divide the number of likes and comments you get by the number of the followers you have. Each industry has different engagement rates but the average global engagement rate on Instagram is around 4.7%, so you might want to set this number as one of your KPIs (key performance indicators) or goals.

Building your brand on Instagram can be quite difficult, but with this guide you will be able to cross over all the hurdles you will face. Just remember to take it one step at a time. Keep building gradually until you get to your goal.

Chapter 12: Tips For Creating High-Quality Content For Your Instagram

How to Create the Perfect Pictures for Your Instagram Business Page

There are millions of pictures and videos being shared on Instagram every day. So, with this being said, how can you stand out and attract users to engage in your post?

The answer? Perfect content!

But in laymen's terms, what is perfect content? As a business, you need to portray your company as something organized, well-made, and well-thought-of. This can reflect on the pictures and videos you upload, so you have to make sure that your content has good composition, great colors, and tones, and is well-lit. Your choice of filter and effects play a huge part too!

Sounds like the job of a professional photographer or photo editing expert? Not really. By the end of this chapter, you're likely to be someone who can produce professional-looking content without having to go through photography class or spending hours trying to understand how photo and video editing works

Tips to Creating the Perfect Picture

Get Good Lighting

Making sure that you're getting good light is one of the key ingredients of creating the perfect photo for your Instagram business. No matter what kind of picture you are trying to capture, there's no amount of filter that can rescue a poor-lit picture.

As much as possible, use natural light as your source. So, if you are planning to take pictures outdoors, early morning or late afternoon photoshoots would be the ideal time. These times of the day are when you can get some of the beautiful outputs under natural lights.

Use Strong Colors and Shapes

Nothing can beat a photo with defined colors and shapes as these characteristics can truly make your photos stand out. It's best to choose and focus on an element that will appear large within your frame. By doing this, you will be able to draw your audiences' attention to your content.

Expressing emotion through your photos is also one of the best practices. If you're new to photography, capturing emotions through pictures may take time. But as you do it more often and you keep practicing, it will start coming naturally. Again, you don't have to be an expert to capture the perfect pictures. Just like any other skill, it's something that can be practiced and be good at overtime.

Learn How to Use Editing Apps

There was a time when Instagram users solely depended on the preset Instagram filters to use on their posts. Admittedly, it was cool at that time, but today, with the number of free editing apps that can help you create professional-looking edited pictures, there's no excuse to still use them.

Using these free editing apps, you can easily enhance that look and overall quality of your pictures. Gone are the days you need to learn how to be an expert on Adobe Photoshop to enhance your photos. Some of the user-friendly alternatives can be downloaded right straight to your smartphones. Some of these are VSCO, Snapseed, PicsArt, and RNI Films, but of course, don't be afraid to shop around for the best tools that meet your needs and requirements.

Another good thing about these apps is that they connect you with some of the professionals where you can get inspiration from. For example, VCSO is not only a photo editing app but also a photo-sharing community that aims to encourage people to show their creativity with the use of the apps.

Put Grids to Good Use

Many people look over the benefits offered by simple grids on their phones or cameras, but with the right usage, these grids can give you amazing output. For perfect Instagram shots, properly align all the elements of the pictures using these grids. Turning on the grid features can help you enhance the overall impacts of the picture.

It's important to observe carefully the overlapping elements on the screen in order to find the subjects' midpoint. As soon as you successfully get the center of the pictures, take the picture. Using the grid features can definitely make a huge difference no matter what kind of photography you are trying to achieve.

Use Your Eyes Before Your Lens

One of the biggest misconceptions in photography is that as long as you have high-end cameras, taking great pictures would be a piece of cake – this can't be any more wrong. The truth is, no matter how expensive your gears are, if you don't have good eyes for photography, your photos wouldn't be as great. Similarly, you don't have to own expensive cameras just to take high-quality photos.

To be able to get professional-looking pictures, it's important to train your eyes accordingly. Instead of taking thousands of pictures to get one perfect shot, take your time and learn how to get the best angles and compositions without the use of a lens. Before pressing the shutter, take pictures with your eyes first. By taking your time to observe what you may capture, you will have better ideas of how you can take the perfect pictures.

6. Use the "Less is More" Ideology

For beginners, one of the biggest mistakes they do when editing pictures for their business is over-editing them. And then most of the time, they just end up being so unappealing. To enhance your pictures, a little editing is enough. Keep in mind that you are editing photos to make your products look as it was taken by a professional photographer, you're not taking it to make it as if it was a part of a fiction movie. On top of it, if you are selling products, you don't want to make your products look different from what it looks like in real life or your customer will get disappointed.

What you want is to apply just some basic editing, which includes adjustments with the brightness, contrast, shadows, highlights, and temperature. What you have to be careful of is adjusting the saturation as it can drastically change the output of the photo.

Again, keep it simple and don't go over the top. Although these are just basic editing, going over the top with these adjustments can decrease the overall quality of the pictures. You don't want to lose its natural look. Always compare the edited output to the original pictures so you can easily tell whether or not you went overboard or you just did it right.

Consider Effects or Filters

The beauty of smartphone photo editing tools is that they come with preset filters that you can use with all pictures in order for them to have the same theme or aesthetics. Furthermore, it allows you to create very attractive photos without needing to be an expert.

You can draw the attention of your audience by adding creative filters and effects. Don't be afraid to try them all until you get the output you desire. But then again, try not to use filters to their full intensity. You can always adjust the settings of these filters in order to find the optimum level of outcome. And again, less is more.

It's Always the Quality over Quantity

One high-quality picture is worth more than 10 bad ones. If you think being active on Instagram by uploading consistently is more important than paying more attention to the quality of the picture you are uploading, then you have to know that you are doing things completely wrong! Keep in mind that it's better to spend hours taking a couple of good pictures than spending a few minutes taking hundreds of bad pictures.

9. Practice Makes Perfect

As cliché as it sounds, taking good pictures is skills that can be developed. And just like any other skills, it's something you can hardly achieve overnight. Practice. Don't be afraid to experiment and try not to get frustrated if you are not satisfied with the results you get on your first tries. Keep trying and before you know it, you will have thousands of followers waiting for your next upload.

In order to have the perfect photos for your Instagram business page, being a professional photographer or editor is not necessary. With the help of the tips and tricks above, you can end up with engaging and captivating content that can help you earn thousands of followers.

How to Create the Perfect Videos for Your Instagram Business Page

When it comes to editing videos, it sure sounds more intimidating for many compared to editing simple pictures. It's pretty understandable – after all, unlike a simple picture, a video consists of multiple frames that may have different lighting, contracts, and shadows. But what people didn't know is that it can be as simple as editing photos. You just have to make sure that you edit your videos matching your branding by adding texts, adjusting its brightness, and cropping it accordingly.

Today, adding videos for their business accounts is no longer only for big brands, any startup business can easily produce high-quality videos that can help them generate more engagement. You also don't need to spend a lot of money to hire a professional to do things for you. You can do it on your phone using free apps.

7.2.1 Tips to Creating the Perfect Picture

When we hear "Instagram aesthetic", the first thing that might come to your mind are attractive photos, professionally made presets, and appealing filters. But with the benefits Instagram video brings, it's important to make the most of it by applying this aesthetic to your videos as well.

It's amazing how there's no limit to what you can do with the videos you can upload on Instagram – main reasons why more and more people, whether the business account or not, are fond of using them.

Everything including Stories, GIFs, and Boomerangs are considered as video content on Instagram. This means that regardless of what type of multi-frame content you're posting, you want to make sure that you've got the right set of tools in creating high-quality video content for your Instagram.

Producing captivating videos for Instagram is one of the most efficient Instagram marketing tactics there are. Videos can be anywhere from 3 to 60 seconds long or longer if you want to upload the video on IGTV and could be uploaded straight from your phone, or by sending the files onto your phone from another source like a computer. This offers you a great amount of flexibility when it comes to using video content in improving your strategy for Instagram marketing.

Today, there's no denying to the fact that video content is the most shared type of content on the platform as it offers the brands an extremely appealing means to market as they tell more about the products. But then again, producing a share-worthy video on Instagram involves some efforts and brainstorming.

In this chapter, you will also learn some of the most practical and tactical ways to plan and shoot Instagram videos for better output and gather more views and engagement. You will also learn some of the examples of different types of Instagram videos you can try to make and upload.

Just like any other aspect of Instagram marketing campaigns, you will want to start the process of creating videos with a clear goal and a well-developed plan.

Setting Clear Goals

Telling a story in just 30 seconds can be a challenge for many. That's why taking your time in planning and conceptualizing a compelling video is extremely important. Before getting started, it's important to ask yourself what your main goals are for sharing the videos. Do you want to gain new followers? To make sales? Or maybe you want people to check out your website?

It's important to be specific. The feel and the tone of the video you are trying to create will depend on the reason as to why you are creating it in the first place.

Tell a Story

Creating a video that tells a story is the more effective way to gain attention and engagement on Instagram as a business. You don't have to make a storyboard for this, but by planning out the video well, you can assure that you will be able to use every second optimally. Doing this will help you manage your time properly and organize the storyline better.

You have to remember that Instagram videos start playing automatically when the user scrolls down their feeds, so it's important to start your video with an attention-grabbing scene. Starting your video this way is going to help it stand out, and more importantly, it's going to capture the interest of the viewer and convince them to watch the whole video to finish the story. But of course, the middle and the end parts of the video have to be strong as well.

At the end of the video, you may want to include call-to-action wherein you can ask the viewer to engage in the content or take action to learn more about your brand.

Lastly, you have to remember that videos on Instagram play in silent unless the user chooses to tap the video to enable the sound. So, you may also want to consider adding on-screen options.

Proper Lighting for Your Video

Just like when you are editing pictures, you don't need to invest in expensive lighting equipment in order to have fantastically well-lit video output. Choosing the settings is always the key, but using some basic technique can also help dramatically. Here are some tips to remember:

Use natural light sources. As much as possible, shoot during the daytime when the sun is out and shining. And it's better if it's outdoors. However, if you're shooting indoors, try to shoot it near the windows and make sure to keep the light in front of you and shining in your direction.

Avoid shooting under overhead lights. Doing this can cause some very poor visual effects. Seek other sources of light and help your subject is moving around until you get to find a good light source.

Use your creativity! If ever your lighting setup isn't doing you any favor, this is when you have to wring your creative juice. If you want to soften the light, you can use a white poster board or even a simple paper to be your reflector. Similarly, if you're aiming to block some unwanted light source, you can use black plastic to cover it.

Shooting the video

Choosing what camera to use for shooting your video is the first thing you need to do. It's best to use the camera directly from your smartphone or DSLR instead of the camera function within the Instagram app. This is because the app's camera has some limitations when it comes to shooting capabilities.

After choosing the camera to use, the next step is shooting the video! Here are some pointers to help you as you start shooting your Instagram videos for your business.

Always shoot the video in portrait for Story or landscape mode for Feed. Thankfully, it didn't take long before Instagram realized that cropping videos and photos into a square is not the best idea they came up with for the platform. This means you can decide as to what orientation you want to upload in. For uploading normal content, it's best to upload it in a landscape, while stories are best taken in portrait. This is because playing Stories will give you a full-screen view while a typical video on the feed doesn't do that. Setting the orientations these ways will give the users full views of the video while playing.

Keep the focus on the subject. Make sure that the device you are using is consistently focusing on the subject. When using your smartphone to shoot the video, you can simply tap the screen on the area where you want it to focus. On the other hand, if you are using a DSLR, you might have to adjust the lens to get it focused on the subject.

Keep the shot steady. Unless you are trying to shoot an indie or a horror film, you'll want to keep the shot steady. You can use a tripod if you are shooting a video in the same frame. On the other hand, if you are shooting a video where you have to move, then you can use a stabilizer like a gyro device.

Be picky. Depending on where you are planning to upload your video, it can be as short as 10 seconds up to 60 seconds or more if you're planning to upload it on IGTV, but then again, because there's a limit to how long you can play the video, you must be selective about what you will include in the video. When editing the video, ask yourself if the scenes you will include are worth being in the video.

Choosing the Content to Upload

There are some categories that will help you to decide on what type of content to upload. These categories include a brand image, types of products, and the story you want to portray in your video.

From there, you can start brainstorming. List down all the ideas you have relevant to the subject and format that you think will help you create a compelling video for your business. Lastly, you have to make sure that the content you make fits the theme and tone for your brand. Again, you must remember that consistency is a very important thing.

Below are different types of video content you can upload on your Instagram. Check the list carefully and find out which types of content you think is the one that will match your marketing goals.

Product details

Show your followers the products you are selling and why they should buy them. Uploading videos that show your products and their features a couple of times a week is ideal. Doing this will be a great complement to uploading lifestyle photos and videos. Uploading this type of videos will provide your followers with an insight into what your brand embodies.

Product-in-action

If you want to break up the monotonous series of staged images on your feed, uploading product-in-action videos would be a great solution. Your followers will not want to see a series of showroom stock photos on your feed.

When you are trying to determine what video to create for product-in-action, you must consider your audience and what gives them inspirations. What kind of customers to do they have and what do they really want? Put yourself in their shoes and look at your brand from a different point of view.

Sneak previews

Are you about to release a new product? If so, announce the news with a teaser video that gives your followers a sneak peek at the new product you're about to launch. By intensifying the hype and excitement surrounding your new release, you'll make your followers think, wonder, and daydream about your product before its even available.

Behind-the-scenes

Behind-the-scenes or BTS for short is video content that is good for building a more personal connection with your followers. When you introduce yourself and your team to your audience, you are giving them backdoor access to how you operate your brand. This will also give you an opportunity to communicate with your audience in an authentic way and generate an intimate connection with them.

Here are some of the themes you can consider uploading in your BTS video:

A day in the life. This will show your followers what a typical day at work in your office looks like.

A tour within your office, warehouse, or studio. Many of your followers are surely curious about what your work station looks like. Show them where you work.

Special events. If you have a product launch or other company events, bring your followers backstage.

Staff introductions. Introducing your followers to the staff and employees will surely give them a different level of trust in your brand knowing that you are more than willing to introduce the identity of the people working in the brand.

Work in action. Show how you create the product and how you put up things together to come up with high-quality products that you are selling to them.

Tutorials

Entertain your followers by showing them how to use your product properly – not only entertaining but also instructive. You can also add humor to your video – people love it!

Series

If you are planning to upload videos that are more than one minute long, you can create a series that break up the whole thing in 60-minute segments. Uploading interesting video content will make your followers ask for more. This will help you gain new followers and more engagement.

Videos on loop

Known as Boomerang, Instagram now uses looping videos like what Vine had. This is when the video automatically starts and repeats in a loop. This is a good way to showcase a fun way to show your products and their features.

Consider using looping videos to showcase a fun or versatile product feature.

Stop motion videos

You need to use an editing app to create this kind of video. And to shoot this, you need to take individual photos of each frame using your camera. And with the help of a stop motion editing up, you can stitch the videos together to create great video content for your Instagram.

Time-lapse videos

This kind of video is popularly used when filming a scenery wherein there's a continuous movement. Most of today's smartphone offers this feature. However, if the phone or camera you are using doesn't have this feature, there are, of course, apps you can install in your phone to edit a video and turn it into a time-lapse one.

If you don't know already, time-lapse videos are condensed longer videos, this means filming a short time-lapse video will take a long time to do. Because of this, it's recommended to use a tripod to mount your camera with. If you're filming using your phone, you might want to set it into airplane mode to make sure that your filming wouldn't get interrupted by incoming calls and texts.

As you can see, you have several options when it comes to choosing the kind of video to upload on your business profile. But in order to come up with a compelling video for your marketing strategy, there are some important points you need to keep in mind: plan early, take your time and consider your followers' goals and lifestyles.

Conclusion

Thank you again for the purchase of this book. In this book you learned what Instagram was, how to use it, and tips on making your money work for you. The marketing business can be tricky, and it takes guidance to navigate. Hopefully, this book gave you that guidance.